Atheism for Christians

Atheism for Christians

Are there lessons for the religious world from the secular tradition?

BENJAMIN T. JONES

WIPF & STOCK · Eugene, Oregon

ATHEISM FOR CHRISTIANS
Are There Lessons for the Religious World from the Secular Tradition?

Copyright © 2016 Benjamin T. Jones. All rights reserved. Except for brief quotations in critical publications or reviews, no part of this book may be reproduced in any manner without prior written permission from the publisher. Write: Permissions, Wipf and Stock Publishers, 199 W. 8th Ave., Suite 3, Eugene, OR 97401.

Wipf and Stock Publishers
199 W. 8th Ave., Suite 3
Eugene, OR 97401

www.wipfandstock.com

ISBN 13: 978-1-4982-2582-3
HB ISBN 13: 978-1-4982-2584-7

Cataloging-in-Publication data:

Jones, Benjamin T., 1982–

    Atheism for Christians : are there lessons for the religious world from the secular tradition? / Benjamin T. Jones.

    xii + 178 p.; 23 cm—Includes bibliographical references and index.

    ISBN 13: 978-1-4982-2582-3
    HB ISBN 13: 978-1-4982-2584-7

    1. Christianity and atheism. 2. Secular humanism. I. Title.

BR128.A8 J66 2016

Manufactured in the USA.

Contents

Preface vii
Acknowledgements xi

1. Why I Am Not an Atheist (but think they get a lot right) 1
2. Atheism and the Question "Why?" 11
3. Atheism and Sex 28
4. Atheism and Tolerance 42
5. Atheism and Ethics 67
6. Atheism and Science 80
7. Atheism and Women 96
8. Atheism and the System 110
9. Atheism and Clannishness 124
10. Atheism and the Politics of Fear 134
11. Conclusion 148

Bibliography 161
Name/Subject Index 173
Scripture Index 176

Preface

THIS BOOK HAS CHANGED beyond recognition since I sat down to write it in 2010 at the historic Hotel Kurrajong in Canberra. With the ghost of Ben Chifley lurking in the corridors, I set out to write an essay titled *Why I Am Not an Atheist* as a refutation of Bertrand Russell's classic text, *Why I Am Not a Christian*. I was a student at the Australian National University and spent the long hours of the day (and usually the small hours of the night as well) immersed in Australian and Canadian colonial history research. I had received a three year postgraduate scholarship and was frantically trying to complete my doctoral thesis before those precious funds ran out. Happily, the thesis was completed in time and eventually became my second book, *Republicanism and Responsible Government*.

While it may seem odd, I began writing this book as a way of unwinding and relaxing from writing my thesis. It was a therapeutic exercise and an escape from the stress and pressure of my academic duties. The following pages and the research they contain were written not for career advancement, but because I felt, and still feel, there are vital conversations that must be had in the Christian world. It also proved a cathartic exercise as I was able to map my own religious and philosophic beliefs that had been gradually evolving for a decade or more. Beyond that, I hoped I could offer something to a crucial debate about Christianity and modernity. Has this ancient religion outlived its usefulness? I remain convinced, it has not.

Motivated by the ubiquitous presence of new atheism, I originally wanted to write what would have been a reasonably standard Christian apologia. I attended the ANU's student-led Atheism Week and found myself wanting to reply to the blunt Hitchens-inspired mantra that "religion poisons everything." At the time, my thinking was heavily influenced by

Preface

Ravi Zacharias and I wanted to use my expertise as a historian and my experience in the academy to offer an apologia that was measured and logical. I hoped to serve as a reminder that thinking people can also be people of faith.

After writing the first few chapters on rather standard topics, (origins of the universe, good and evil, religion and science) I decided to write a chapter titled, "An Olive Branch: What Atheists Get Right." I thought it was important to approach these questions not from a combative position but one of deep thought and discussion. As such, it seemed only right to happily acknowledge the outstanding contribution to humanity from the secular tradition. The more I wrote, the more I wanted to write and it soon became apparent that this should be a book rather than a chapter. The secular pantheon contains many of the brightest minds in history and my conviction firmed that their stories should be read and understood by Christians as well as atheists.

Christianity is such a broad church and I am very conscious that this book may seem like little more than an attack on traditional, conservative attitudes and a call for progressive renewal. I can only hope that readers believe me when I say I come to these topics as a friend, not an enemy of Christianity. Like the great scientist and philosopher who is discussed in this work, Karl Popper, I am "anything else but an opponent of religion." This is not a call to convert but simply a call to think. There is so much beauty and wisdom in the Bible and in the Christian message and I have been blessed to see some of it firsthand. My parents began a ministry called Jesus Cares and have spent the last twenty-five years providing food—and, far more importantly, friendship—to the homeless community on the streets of Sydney. This is Christianity at its best; selfless, sacrificial, and full of love. I believe the great tragedy of our times is that the modern church is caricatured as a closed-minded institution that uses a religious guise to cloak bigotry and prejudice. Even in the relativist maze of postmodernity, I am convinced that Christianity still has much to offer the world.

I have personally been inspired and provoked by the ideas and contributions of great secular thinkers and I believe all thinking Christians should be aware of their place in history and engaged with their arguments and insights. This does not at all mean that traditional faith must be abandoned. One does not have to accept an idea in order to understand it. The Christian church should be confident enough to engage with ideas from other traditions and brave enough to look honestly at its own teachings in order to abandon what is bad, change what is outdated, and cling to what is good. That is the challenge of this book and my heart-felt hope is that it is read and received in the spirit in which it was written.

The Bible says that: "Happy is the man that findeth wisdom, and the man that getteth understanding. For the merchandise of it is better than the merchandise of silver, and the gain thereof than fine gold. She is more precious than rubies: and all the things thou canst desire are not to be compared unto her" (Prov 3:13–15). Great thoughts and ideas should always be respected and considered. It should not matter where that wisdom and knowledge comes from. With the call to knowledge ringing true, I offer this little volume.

Benjamin T. Jones
Penrith, Australia
13 March 2015

Acknowledgements

IT IS A WONDERFUL thing indeed to be able to teach and write about the topics I love. This book, like my others, is the end product of much hard work and deep thought and I owe a debt of gratitude to a number of people for seeing it through to completion. My thanks go firstly to the wonderful staff at Wipf and Stock for seeing something of value in my writing and for their ongoing support and impeccable professionalism. In particular, thanks to my meticulous editor, Robin Parry. I also must thank my colleagues at Western Sydney University and the staff at the State Library of New South Wales. Many friends have kindly looked over parts of this book, but I must acknowledge in particular the helpful comments and suggestions of Micaela MacLachlan and Nicholas Andrew. My parents, Robyn and John Jones have been my life-long cheerleaders, editors, and financial backers. I thank them for supporting my academic endeavors and for being unwavering exemplars of the beauty in Christian faith. My deepest thanks go to my precious wife. Her love and sacrifices allow me to achieve otherwise impossible things.

It is a blessing indeed to live in a free country and to be able to discuss important issues without fear of punishment or persecutions. Millions of people around the world face violence, imprisonment, or death if they challenge the dominant religious structures of their society. To live in a time and place where Christianity can be freely discussed, critiqued, or rejected, I am grateful. I am humbly aware that the freedom I enjoy is an inheritance from free-thinkers and dissenters throughout the ages who endured hardship and inquisition rather than forfeit their right to challenge the system. I hope we remain ever vigilant and always ready to defend free speech—even speech we do not like. I truly believe that the open exchange of ideas and the ability to disagree without violence or malice, is what makes a society truly great.

1

Why I Am Not an Atheist
(but think they get a lot right)

When Melbourne played host to the Global Atheist Convention in 2010 and again in 2012, it was, for the most part, a gathering like any other. These events happen all the time. Every year there are conventions for historians, scientists, boating enthusiasts, medical practitioners, retirees, tax consultants, and, of course, religions, both traditional and new age. The format is generally the same. A function room and keynote speakers are booked, delegates pay a fee, presentations are made, and then mountains of books, DVDs, and other resources are sold. Unlike the myriad of other events, the Global Atheist Convention managed to attract fierce opposition and protesters. In scenes that were almost comical, groups of Islamic and Christian protesters rallied outside the Melbourne Convention Centre to warn participants that they were bringing down the wrath of the God they do not believe in. Watching video footage of the heated shouting competitions between indignant theists and defiant anti-theists, I could not help but find a certain ridiculousness to it all.[1] Why were these protesters so offended that others did not share their views? Also, why are the same people not protesting Sexpo or the Mind Body Spirit Festival? Both of those high

---

1. Scores of amateur videos showing the different protests at the Global Atheist Convention are easily accessed on Youtube.com.

profile events promote a lifestyle and philosophy at odds with fundamental Islam or Christianity. Why is atheism in particular the target of such outrage?

Atheism and Christianity are obviously different worldviews, but I strongly challenge the notion that they are the natural enemies often presented. Is there no common ground? Is there no basis for civility and diversity? The BBC One discussion show, *The Big Questions*, ran a fascinating episode asking if it was time for all religions to accept evolution. The panel was not split, as one might expect, between atheistic scientists who promote evolution and religious leaders who reject it. Rather the pro-evolution case was presented jointly and passionately by science writer and atheist Matt Ridley and Christian palaeontologist Robert Asher. Also making the case was the geneticist and atheist Steve Jones and the Anglican Reverend Malcolm Brown. The divide on that panel was not between Christianity and atheism but reason and blind Fundamentalism. It was a debate between thinking people and those who insist that through dogmatic observance thinking can be avoided. The tragedy of Fundamentalism is that it denies the historic nexus of faith and reason that has underpinned Christian philosophers and apologists since the time of St. Paul. Christianity was never supposed to require mindless observance and the "celebration of reason" that marks new atheism is not something to challenge Christianity, but rather to improve it.[2]

When St. Peter claimed that all believers must be ready to give an apologia for their faith, he literally meant they should be able to offer a logical answer, grounded in reason (1 Pet 3:15). The word *apologia* comes from the Greek legal system where the prosecution would present a *Kategoria* and the defence would offer an *Apologia*. St. Paul used the word *apologia* to describe his legal defence before Agrippa (Acts 26:2). The central part of apologia is the Greek word *logos*, which forms the root of the English term logic. The Latin form, *ratio*, was translated into French as *raison* and English as reason. Christianity must be able to defend itself academically if it is to survive in an increasingly sceptical, cynical, and educated world. Crucially, the Christian world must have the moral and intellectual courage to abandon long-held traditions and prejudices if they are found to be repugnant to reason.

I am not an atheist, but I am probably not a typical theist either. I grew up amid the Charismatic movement that influenced Australia and

---

2. A "Celebration of Reason" was the theme of the 2012 Global Atheist Convention.

New Zealand in the 1980s. My earliest memories are from the age of four or five where I would pray in tongues with my Dad, engage in spiritual warfare at Sunday School, and frequently rededicate my life to Jesus as I was concerned I may have somehow fallen out of favor. The majority of my childhood and teenage years were spent attending Hills Christian Life Centre (now Hillsong Church), Sydney Christian Outreach Centre (now Sydney International Network of Churches), and various other Assemblies of God churches. While these modern Pentecostal churches were proud to say they rejected "religion" and promoted a personal relationship with Christ, they were as staunchly conservative as traditional churches on most issues. While completing a doctorate in history at the Australian National University, I found myself increasingly attracted to the quiet meditation of the traditional Mass. I put down my electric guitar, which had been my "calling" in Pentecostal circles, and began attending the Roman Catholic parish on campus. Bucking the current trend of Catholics leaving for the modern music and festive atmosphere of modern Evangelicalism, I went the other way and was confirmed in the Catholic Church in 2010. Today I would describe myself as a progressive, free-thinking Christian. While I see enormous beauty and value in Christianity, there is also meanness, bigotry, and a slavish observance to tradition that has made for an awkward adjustment to modernity. Perhaps most damaging of all, is a creeping clannishness that seeks to insulate followers from the outside world. The intension may be to protect from harm, but an inward-looking Christianity cuts off the possibility of learning and being inspired by the richness of other religious traditions and from the secular tradition also.

While my faith is an important part of my identity, my worldview has also been profoundly shaped by many of the great philosophers, some of whom were pantheists, deists, theists, and others still, avowed atheists. I believe all of these schools, and many others besides, have been championed by intellectual giants and offer a great deal of wisdom for the discerning reader. Along with theists, I believe all of these schools, and many others besides, have been championed by intellectual giants and offer a great deal of wisdom for the discerning reader. An appreciation for the history of ideas, the evolution of Western thought, and the architecture of logic and argument can greatly enrich a person. This knowledge gives us a better understanding of the construction and application of our own worldview and that of others. Looking back on the Christian environment I grew up in, I am struck by the defensive tribalism of many churchgoers and their hostility towards this perceived atheistic art called philosophy.

Atheism for Christians

In 2014 the Christian feature film *God's Not Dead* was released, achieving great commercial success, if accompanied by generally negative reviews. The crux of the film rests on an impossibly ludicrous premise where a militant atheist professor demands his philosophy class sign a declaration that "God is dead" or risk failing the course. The star of the film is a faithful Christian who risks his academic career to challenge the professor and ultimately wins him and the entire class over to theism. The fact that the professor's actions grossly violate academic ethics seems completely lost on the writers and much of the conservative Christian audience. No credible university would tolerate a professor questioning or ridiculing the religious beliefs of its students. Ironically, it is not secular state universities but only independent religious ones that insist their students hold certain beliefs. The fact that a faith film could employ such an implausible storyline reveals a great deal about the Christian market. The film is responding to a profound cultural anti-intellectualism and a general suspicion of academics in general and philosophers in particular.

The influential Carthaginian writer, Tertullian, held a similar disdain for philosophy. Considered by some to be the father of Western theology, Tertullian saw philosophy as time wasted with endless questions that could have been spent meditating on the wonder of God. His comments on the death of Thales of Miletus are telling:

> It therefore served Thales of Miletus quite right, when, star-gazing as he walked with all the eyes he had, he had the mortification of falling into a well. . . . His fall, therefore, is a figurative picture of the philosophers; of those, I mean, who persist in applying their studies to a vain purpose, since they indulge a stupid curiosity on natural objects, which they ought rather (intelligently to direct) to their Creator.[3]

Thales of Miletus was a pre-Socratic thinker who is credited by Aristotle as the first philosopher in the Greek tradition.[4] His curiosity about natural phenomena and attempts to understand the natural world without supernatural explanations earned him the praise of subsequent philosophers, but the derision of Tertullian. Christianity has, of course, engaged with philosophy in meaningful ways over the centuries, but a culture of suspicion, if not hostility, towards those seeking answers without recourse

---

3. Tertullian, *The Selected Works of Tertullian*, 242–43.
4. Heit, "Nietzsche's Genealogy of Early Greek Philosophy," 218.

to the Divine has endured. While it certainly does not define Christianity writ large, it is something I have personally encountered.

I remember when I was first accepted to study history and philosophy at university, one of my Christian friends asked in amazement why I would want to study anything other than the Bible. Imagining some inextricable link, many other friends sternly warned me not to let the academy to turn me into an atheist. For these friends, re-reading the Bible over and over was far preferable to studying philosophy and Bible College was seen as the only safe form of tertiary education. As it happens, I never encountered the evangelistic atheists dreamt up by *God's Not Dead*. The only attempts at religious conversion I ever saw came from the campus Christian and Islamic groups (who were both perfectly respectful, simply offering leaflets and often food to any who wanted information). While I never became an atheist, I did fall in love with the academy. The tradition of research and debate, the pursuit of excellence, and the search for truth filled me with wonder as I took my first tentative steps down the corridors of knowledge. Over nine years, I completed four degrees before taking on teaching roles. The academy has become part of my life and I am all the richer for it.

Contrary to some of the fears my friends expressed, it is clearly possible to study philosophy at the highest levels without abandoning deeply held convictions. This is because it is possible to entertain ideas without accepting them. Further, it is possible to study and to learn from great thinkers without necessarily accepting their worldview or ontological premises. While I am not personally an atheist, there is an undeniable power and beauty to the writings of David Hume and Simone de Beauvoir, John Stuart Mill and Karl Marx, Bertrand Russell, and so many others. In 2012 Alain de Botton was able to gaze over the philosophical divide and find plentiful material for his tome *Religion for Atheists*.[5] Similarly, I am convinced that religious people can gain a great deal of insight from a better understanding atheism. Taking a leaf from de Botton, this little volume is titled *Atheism for Christians*. Abraham Lincoln famously said, "though passion may have strained, it must not break our bonds of affection."[6] In an increasingly diverse and globalized society, we should not seek to be enemies but friends with those who hold a different worldview. To this end, the popular presentation of the recent theism versus atheism debates has done little to advance knowledge and has changed the opinions of few.

5. De Botton, *Religion for Atheists*.
6. White Jr., *Lincoln's Greatest Speech*, 76.

Why should Christians be interested in wisdom from the secular tradition? If a worldview is robust and logically sound it should have nothing to fear from other traditions. The aim here is not to convert but to challenge. It takes maturity and a conciliatory spirit to acknowledge the accumulated wisdom from other worldviews and it is certainly no betrayal to question aspects of your own. Whether you believe it is a gift from a creator or the result of evolution, reason is humanity's most paradoxical gift. It is a powerful lantern in the dark and winding alley, but so rarely do we choose to light it. The power of a question is far greater than all the weapons of war; however, it is seldom that we ask, preferring overwhelmingly to swim in the safe waters of tradition. Christianity must have the moral courage to ask tough questions. Why do we believe certain things and act in certain ways? Is the secular world getting things right that we are not? What ideas and practices must be enshrined as canonical and which ones reflect cultural currency and ethics *du jour*? The great heroes of the Christian tradition have been the women and men willing to boldly break with tradition to pursue what is right and what is reasonable. The greatest radical of all was Christ himself, who regularly discarded societal and religious norms. Through debate, scrutiny, and critical evaluation the sweet mask of an idea may be torn off to reveal the monster beneath. All things must be tested.

Between 1256 and 1258 CE the philosopher and theologian St. Thomas Aquinas wrote the *Summa Contra Gentiles*. Becoming the eponymous founder of the Thomistic School, he asserted that many of the most central epistemological truths could be gleaned through natural reason, unaided by divine revelation. At a time when theism in general and Christianity in particular was the dominant European worldview, Aquinas reminded his readers that ideas should be questioned. In his subsequent *magnus opus*, written between 1265 and 1274, *Summa Theologica*, Aquinas drew upon Aristotle as well as other ancient non-Christian scholars. Through natural reason, he recognized the intrinsic truth in religious traditions other than his own. The pantheistic worldview held by some of ancient Greece's famous philosophers had fallen from dominance in Western culture. Only the best parts of the Socratic, Aristotelian, and other schools, the parts undergirded by reason, could survive the cultural *coup d'état*. Should we enter a context where Christianity is no longer the dominant worldview, Aquinas warned, "we must . . . have recourse to the natural reason, to which all men are forced to give their assent."[7] We are now at that point.

---

7. Aquinas, *Summa Contra Gentiles*, 62.

Why I Am Not an Atheist (but think they get a lot right)

Ontology in the popular Western consciousness passed through several significant moods following the time of Aquinas. Of particular note is the Protestant Reformation, the subsequent Roman Catholic Counter-Reformation, the European Enlightenment, the rise of deism, the Great Awakening, and the early formation of Evangelicalism. Yet as diverse as these moods were, and their plethora of subsidiaries and variations, they can all be, however uncomfortably, placed together in the long pews of theism. The anti-theistic worldview, though doubtless present through the ages, did not make much noise in the Western world at a popular level until the later part of the nineteenth century. Even then, its full cultural impact was not readily apparent until the twentieth century. Between the 1950s and 1970s, secularization, particularly in Great Britain and the United States, became a standard academic topic for sociologists and historians. By the mid-1960s it was generally accepted, in the academy at least, that both nations, and many others besides, were essentially secular and that, despite high levels of religious affiliation, the social and cultural significance of Christianity had gradually given way to the process of secularization.[8] In the first decade of the twenty-first century, even the traditional affiliations began to crumble. Today, the Christian worldview for us is akin to the Greek pantheon for Aquinas. No longer the dominant worldview in popular culture, only the best parts are likely to survive.

Although global Christianity is on the rise as a result of sharp growth in Asia and Africa, there has been a steady decline for decades in its traditional Western strongholds. In Great Britain, the number of Christians has dropped sharply from 71.7 to 59.3 percent in the decade from 2001 to 2011.[9] Meanwhile, the number of people citing no religion spiked from 14.3 to 25.1 percent.[10] Over the same period, Australians reporting an affiliation with Christianity dropped from 68 to 61.1 percent, while no religion grew to 22.3 percent.[11] Canada followed a similar trajectory in their 2011 census, with Christianity dropping to 67.3 percent and no religion growing to 23.9 percent.[12] The United States appears to buck the trend with 73

---

8. Brown and Snape, *Secularisation in the Christian World*, 4.
9. "Census Shows Rise in Foreign-Born", *BBC News UK*, 11 December 2012.
10. Ibid.
11. Australian Bureau of Statistics. "Reflecting a Nation: Stories from the 2011 Census," para 21–26.
12. Statistics Canada. "2011 National Household Survey," para 20–26.

percent of the population holding to Christianity of some kind in 2012.¹³ Indeed, 58 percent of Americans say religion is "very important in their lives" compared with 22 percent in Spain, 21 in Germany, 17 in Britain, and just 13 in France.¹⁴ Nevertheless, the United States, like the rest of the Western world, has seen a sharp increase in people claiming no religion at 19.6 percent.¹⁵ The rise of atheism in the twenty-first century and the slow-but-steady decline of Christianity in Europe, North America, and Australasia has certainly led to tensions, especially in the battle for political clout and legitimate use of public and intellectual space. While the media, and indeed many leading protagonists, have presented two incompatible and oppositional worldviews, this book will argue that the hostile Christian/atheist binary represents a false dichotomy. Atheists can learn from the Christian tradition and Christians can learn from atheism.

It is not possible to know how many hours have been spent debating the existence of God or how much ink has been spilled publishing books and articles on the topic. The numbers would be truly extraordinary. In the Western world, the debate is often a philosophical Field of Honor where, either implicitly or explicitly, it is really Christianity and atheism that clash lances. The reason for this is twofold. Firstly, the Western world in the modern era has an intellectual tradition that allows these debates to take place. Secondly, in virtually every Western nation, Christianity was at some point the dominant ideological force, cultural identifier, and shaper of political and social theory. Secularism has largely replaced Christianity in Western public discourses only recently in the grand theatre of history, so it is little surprise that these debates are taking place with such passion and intensity. A great paradigm shift took place in the twentieth century that saw the antitheistic worldview dislodge Christianity from its position of prominence. Now in the twenty-first century we find church leaders fighting to maintain some degree of social standing and a cohort of new atheists seeking to drive theism completely from the public arena. In this heady environment we find also a breed of militant atheists committed to driving religion from even the private sphere with the argument that raising a child as a Christian is a form of child abuse.¹⁶ Clearly, this is a topic that matters.

13. Pew Research Center. "Nones on the Rise."

14. Ibid.

15. Ibid.

16. Christopher Hitchens and Richard Dawkins have both suggested in many interviews and speeches that raising a child as a Christian or with any other religious affiliation is a form of abuse. Hitchens dedicates a chapter in *God is not Great* to the question

Why I Am Not an Atheist (but think they get a lot right)

The contested moniker, new atheism, has been applied with some controversy to a brand of popular philosophy that achieved prominence in the mid-2000s. The prefix "new" is misleading as the arguments put forward are generally modern adaptations of anti-theistic arguments that have been espoused since the time of Friedrich Nietzsche (1844–1900) and before. The newness of the new atheism is revealed in the level of open hostility towards religion and the scorn and invective readily displayed for those who dare disagree with the thesis put forward in a series of bestselling books. In 2004 Sam Harris released *The End of Faith*, a tome highly critical of religion in the wake of 9/11 and the age of terrorism. In 2006, Richard Dawkins' *God Delusion* and Daniel Dennett's *Breaking the Spell* were released. The following year, the late Christopher Hitchens published *God is Not Great: How Religion Poisons Everything*. Together, the quartet self-identified as the four horsemen of atheism. Christian apologists and other theistic thinkers rushed to denounce these and the many other products of the new atheists. Alister McGrath responded specifically to Dawkins in his 2007 work, *The Dawkins Delusion?* The next year saw Edward Feser publish a more general criticism of the new atheists titled *The Last Superstition*. Douglas Wilson went on a debating tour with Christopher Hitchens challenging his claim that religion poisons everything. Their public exchanges culminated in a book and the 2009 documentary, *Collision: Is Christianity Good for the World?* In the turbulent first decade of the twenty-first century, numerous other books, articles, and lectures appeared both advocating and denouncing the new atheism.

The new atheists and their Christian apologist counterparts engage in intellectual warfare, not to learn from each other, not even with the hope of converting one another, but with the aim of electrifying their own support base. Both sides display a stunning hypocrisy when they denounce the violence committed by one side while ignoring their own violent past. A philosophy must never be judged on its abuses. This is the cardinal sin of propagandists. Whenever the Spanish Inquisition or Crusades are used as evidence of the inherent violence within the Christian faith you can be sure a fair discussion is not forthcoming. This line of reasoning has the same merit as using Stalinist Russia or Maoist China as an archetype atheist society—that is to say, none at all. Those of the "religion poisons everything"

"Is Religion Child Abuse?" Dawkins' most famous quote on the subject is, "Who will say with confidence that sexual abuse is more permanently damaging to children than threatening them with the eternal and unquenchable fires of hell?" Richard Dawkins, "Quotes."

school must wilfully put their heads in the sand and ignore the mountainous evidence of religiously inspired acts of kindness and charity. Equally so, Christians generally, but Christian apologists more specifically, are wrong to dismiss atheism as utterly hedonistic, nihilistic, and devoid of value.

Although many would cringe at the metaphor, atheism is a broad church. Or, to move away from religious imagery, it is a philosophy/worldview/ideology/concept with a diverse group of adherents. As with Christianity, and religious people of all stripes, atheism has its fundamentalists. These aggressive evangelists are completely intolerant of different views and only feel really comfortable around like-minded people. Atheism, again like all religions, has committed adherents who are comfortable in their belief system and see no need to have it imposed on others, nor is it a barrier to friendly and rewarding interactions with those who hold to other ideas. Happily this is the majority. Far from a foe to be bested, there is much religious people can learn from atheism. At its best, it is a philosophy that champions critical thinking, thoughtful deliberation, and an inquisitive nature—all laudable traits.

The following chapters highlight some of the best aspects of atheistic thought and some of the great thinkers in the atheist tradition. They are not presented as authoritative. It should not be presumed that I fully endorse any of the works discussed, only that I find them worthy of contemplation. It is hoped that this work will find some middle ground and particularly that Christians will be able to acknowledge, if not accept, some of the value and wisdom to be found in other places. This book is not a call to conversion but simply a call to thinking. The world itself is a living library full of valuable lessons for the discerning reader. Consciously or unconsciously, we all must tackle the great Socratic riddle, how best shall we live? Just as there are religious practices and ideas that may still appeal to avowed atheists, there is much in the atheist tradition that can be beneficial to Christians. The Bible says that "wisdom is better than rubies; and all the things that may be desired are not to be compared to it" (Prov 8:11). As a Christian, I take that as a call to explore the works of the great thinkers and to glean what you can. Presented here is atheism for Christians.

2

Atheism and the Question "Why?"

THE 2012 GLOBAL ATHEIST Convention in Melbourne opened with a spectacular video that described the question *why* as "one word that just might be the most powerful force in all existence."[1] The "obnoxious" reply offered by religious people is simply because God made it so. It is only the brave few who keep alive this power by refusing to accept "such a narrow answer to such complex questions." The video then depicts a timeline of magnificent thinkers who asked the question why. Naturally the video does not want to highlight the many Christian scientists and intellectuals who also asked the question why and made significant contributions to knowledge. Irrespective of the crude binary that places atheism, science, and rational thought on one side and religion, ignorance, and blind faith on the other; the point of the video is still valid. We should, indeed must, ask *why*. We must do it all the time. And we certainly must ask ourselves why we believe what we do before bothering others with our ideas.

The irony with this presentation is that the question *why* has been central to Christian thinking since the religion began. The meetings of the early church leaders, the compilation and production of the Latin Vulgate, the Reformation and Counter-Reformation, right up to the Second Vatican Council have all been driven by the question *why*. Some Christian

1. Atheist Foundation. "Opening Video—2012 Global Atheist Convention."

Atheism for Christians

Fundamentalists act and speak as though the full canon of Christian works and tradition was magically dropped from heaven without the process of human interpretation, rational thought, and critical thinking. For centuries Christian thinkers have asked *why*. Why do we think the way we do? Why do we follow the practices we follow? Why do we believe what we believe? The rise of atheism should serve as a reminder to Christians that academic curiosity and a questioning mind is natural to humanity. It is how we have survived. It is something to embrace, not to run from.

Modern Christianity, especially Evangelicalism, has been notoriously closed for theological and even ethical debate. Despite its revisionist origins in the early eighteenth century, modern Evangelicals, like the Charismatic Pentecostals and other new denominations, have been profoundly shaped by the late nineteenth- and early twentieth-century Fundamentalist movement in the United States. Fundamentalist Christianity is, by its very nature, opposed to debate. It insists that certain principles are fundamental to the Christian faith and therefore cannot be challenged or adapted. Meeting in Niagara, New York in 1895, a conference of conservative Protestants agreed on five principles of the Christian faith, including, "the literal inerrancy of the Bible, the divinity of Jesus Christ, the virgin birth, a substitutionary theory of atonement, and the physical resurrection and bodily return of Christ."[2] Twelve tracts defending the fundamentals were freely and widely distributed in throughout the 1910s and in 1919 a powerful World's Christian Fundamentalist Association was formed.[3] Although there was a diversity of voices, particular stress was placed on the first fundamental. The widespread insistence that the Bible be read as literally true (including six day creation) was a direct response to the rise of Darwinian science and the growing acceptance of evolution by natural selection over millions of years among the scientific and broader community. Although science and religion have a checkered relationship, many of the great scientific minds throughout the centuries have been practising Christians. Fundamentalism viewed science and the academy more generally with suspicion. Seen as a direct assault on Christianity, the role of reason was diminished. In its place, followers were encouraged to simply accept the fundamentals on faith.

American journalist and critic of religion Henry Louis Mencken was scathing of the anti-intellectual culture that developed in some Christian

2. Chryssides, *Historical Dictionary of New Religious Movements*, 144.
3. Marsden, *Understanding Fundamentalism and Evangelicalism*, 57.

believe, not only that are all non-Christians are wrong, but that the other two billion Christians in the world are all misreading the Bible and incorrectly categorizing good and evil. While Christianity will always have intellectual space for absolutes it should acknowledge that the vast majority of issues that confront people are not in this sphere. Christians must find their own path through the ethical challenges of life, not only in the many instances where the Bible is silent, but in the contested areas where it is not.

Perhaps the focus should not be on endlessly categorizing and separating sin and non-sin, righteousness and wickedness, but simply attempting to do the most good we can. Doing good can be a fraught concept for many Christians as a theology has been built up that tends to condemn rather that congratulate it. Although something of a distortion of the Reformers, within Evangelicalism especially, good works are often viewed with suspicion, as a person could be "fooled" into thinking works are enough to gain salvation. The point is made with urgency that good people will go to hell if they have not accepted Christ as their personal Lord and Savior. Choo Thomas is a Korean American author who claims to have visited both heaven and hell on several occasions. In *Heaven Is So Real*, which has sold over a million copies, she recounts being devastated after visiting hell. She writes that God said to her:

> The reason I am showing this to you, My daughter, is so you will fully understand that no matter how good people are, they will go to Hell if they do not accept me. . . . I know your parents and friends were good people in many ways, but they were not saved. That's why this is the only place for them. It is here that they will have to spend eternity.[28]

Whatever one makes of this story, and the many other people who claim to have returned from heaven or hell, the theological basis is widespread. Indeed, the glowing foreword to Thomas' book is written by the pastor of the world's largest church, Dr. David Yonggi Cho of Yoido Full Gospel Church.[29] Salvation, of course, is central to Christianity, but the caricature of well-intentioned missionaries handing out Bibles to starving children rings true if the place of good works is denigrated. In terms of practical ethics, the best of the secular tradition can motivate us to do what good we can.

---

28. Choo, *Heaven Is So Real*, 52.
29. Ibid., xxvi.

Atheism for Christians

While "the good" is a philosophical concept in itself that can stir fierce debate, most people would accept Peter Singer's statement that, all things being equal, "a world with less suffering and more happiness" would be better.[30] Singer's ethical challenge is to be an effective altruist. In his 2015 work, *The Most Good You Can Do*, he champions "a philosophy and social movement which applies evidence and reason to working out the most effective ways to improve the world."[31] Effective altruism is difficult because so often we want to give to charities that appeal to our emotions or that line up with our religious inclinations. Some of us may give small donations to many charities throughout the year because the act itself makes us feel good. Few investigate the administration costs and seek out the most efficient. Many ignore the fact that processing costs may negate nearly the entire sum of a small gift and that a single large donation to an effective charity would do far more good. Most people will feel a greater emotional urge to help rebuild homes in a nearby area which has been affected by bushfires than to help unknown children in a far off country whose lives could be saved by the same donation. Similarly, some Christians may be opposed to supporting charities that provide condoms to Africa despite this being one of the most effective way to combat the spread of HIV/AIDS. Effective altruism, and Singer's work more generally, argues that binary logic is unsuitable and often unhelpful when determining a course of action. An effective ethical framework must be fluid, must acknowledge the full range of factors that surround the action, and, above all, must be grounded in reason at the expense of feeling.

The secular tradition does not try to give itself false authority but defers always to logic and reason. With the hegemony of Christian morality demonstrably broken in the West, churches cannot rely on cultural capital to enforce its traditions but must compete on an even footing in the marketplace of ideas. Secular ethics are changeable. To follow the Nietzschean parable, we invent our own sacred games and we are free to change the rules and create new ones as our society evolves and changes. The influential economists and outspoken atheist John Maynard Keynes reportedly put it this way, "When the facts change, I change my mind. What do you do, sir?"[32] This concept is particularly disturbing to Christian thinkers who champion the idea of universal, unchangeable, objective moral laws. De-

30. Singer, *The Most Good You Can Do*, 7.
31. Ibid., 4–5.
32. Kiser, *Beyond Right and Wrong*, 354.

spite this, Christian ethics have changed throughout the centuries and even decades. Attitudes towards slavery and women are two obvious examples. Indeed, Bible verses were used to both promote and oppose slavery. Even today, the Bible is used to argue both that women and men are equal and that women are subject to their husbands and not permitted to be in authority over a man.

Life is complicated and no two journeys are ever the same. While we can learn from each other's examples and experiences, no two decisions will ever be identical and we must all take responsibility for our choices. While the traditional Christian framework favors deontological ethics and a categorical right and wrong, it would do well to study the secular tradition also. The circumstances, background, motives, and outcome of any action must be considered along with the action itself. Atheist thinkers are quick to acknowledge that their ethical positions are subjective and the net result of an honest attempt to navigate a difficult decision guided by reason. Christianity would do well to take a similar approach. The Bible is full of wisdom, but it is not a complete, clear, and definitive set of rules for every situation in life. Most of the positions Christians take individually and collectively are the product of discussion and reason, not divine revelation. Accepting this will not only make Christianity more accessible and relevant to those outside its walls, it will also free adherents to think for themselves and to take responsibility for their own ethical outlook. Albert Einstein once said, "I consider ethics to be an exclusively human concern with no superhuman authority behind it."[33] Christians are traditionally very good at deferring to divine moral authority. Practical ethics without any supernatural guidance is also necessary and the secular tradition offers many valuable examples.

33. Einstein, *The Human Side*, 39.

6

Atheism and Science

THE STINGING IRONY IN the false dichotomy of religion versus science is that religious people around the world have contributed so much to the advancement of scientific knowledge. Islamic and Christian scientists in particular have greatly shaped Western civilization and have unlocked wisdom to benefit all humanity. Religion and science have been disentangled over the past two centuries to create a method of natural inquiry, free from outside influence or bias. The modern scientific method allows researchers to follow the evidence wherever it leads them, free from fear. This development has hardly made religion redundant. Rather, it has clarified the intellectual spheres where religion and science operate. Science will only comment on matters where evidence can be tested and logical conclusions drawn. It cannot comment on art or beauty, for instance. A computer will never be able to judge a painting or a song. Science can create weapons, but cannot determine the ethics of their use.

In his 2011 work, *The Brain is Wider Than the Sky: Why Simple Solutions Don't Work in a Complex World*, Bryan Appleyard makes the case that science has limits and can never fully unlock the mystery of existence. The author certainly does not to say science can go no further, but keenly observes that with every discovery the human brain reveals itself to be more complex and unsearchable. Christianity has nothing to fear from science, but must be respectful of the theoretic boundaries that separate the two. When Christian ideas or biblical conclusions are applied *a priori* to the scientific method, an artificial and pyrrhic battle takes place. It is from these faith-based skirmishes that the crude stereotype of religion versus reason emerges and gains currency. Ultimately, the reputation of Christianity is damaged when adherents show contempt towards science and the collective wisdom of the academy.

An honest investigation must be able to separate propaganda and ideology from science and religion. The object of propaganda is to convince as many people as possible that a certain position or worldview is true with complete indifference to its truthfulness. Some religion is clearly guilty of being propaganda. There are people who use religion to exploit people, to make money and have little concern whether what they teach is true or not. What is often forgotten, however, is that science can just as easily be manipulated for propaganda purposes. Funded by large tobacco conglomerates, many scientists argued passionately against the evidence that linked smoking with cancer, long after a medical consensus was reached. Naomi Oreskes and Erik M. Conway note that "by the late 1970s, scores of lawsuits had been filed claiming personal injury from smoking cigarettes, but the industry had successfully defended itself by using scientists as expert witnesses to testify that the smoking-cancer link was not unequivocal."[1] Why was this done? For the same reason that motivates religious charlatans: greed. Humans are fallible, corruptible, and susceptible to all manner of temptation. Be that as it may, genuine science and genuine religion share a common goal. They are both honest attempts to understand the world and to arrive at some sort of truth as to how and why things are the way they are.

While atheistic zealots insist we must decide whether we believe in science or religion, this is a demonstrably false dichotomy. The myth that the two are mutually exclusive is exposed not only in the fact that they deal with fundamentally different questions about life but also in basic differences in approach. Owing much gratitude to the English Renaissance philosopher, Francis Bacon, modern science is based on repeatable experiments. Rigorous and continual experimentation will ultimately establish or discredit a scientific theory. If an experiment produces the same results

---

1. They go on to make the obvious comparison to the handful of scientist, usually employed by the oil and coal industries, who go against the overwhelming consensus and argue that the link between climate change and human actions is not unequivocal. Oreskes and Conway, *Merchants of Doubt*, 13.

numerous times in a controlled scientific setting with limited variables, then certain conclusions can be logically inferred. For all the aspects of human life that can be enhanced through science, it cannot tell us how to live. We do not have hundreds of lives with which to conduct experiments. We have one life only. We do not live in a controlled scientific setting with limited variables. We live in a rich mosaic of cultures, creeds, and ideas. The scientific method simply cannot be applied to human existence. We do not stand in a laboratory with infinite time and resources at our disposal. We stand like a footballer, staring down the goal keeper, preparing to take a penalty kick. We do not know if it will be a goal, a save, or a miss. All we know is we have one shot only.

Science and religion ask different questions and take a fundamentally different approach to answering them. Great scientists throughout history have expressed all forms of religious belief. Eminent evolutionary biologist, Stephen Jay Gould, wrote in the *Scientific American* in 1992:

> Darwin himself was agnostic (having lost his religious beliefs upon the tragic death of his favorite daughter), but the great American botanist Asa Gray, who favored natural selection and wrote a book entitled Darwiniana, was a devout Christian. Move forward 50 years: Charles D. Walcott, discoverer of the Burgess Shale fossils, was a convinced Darwinian and an equally firm Christian, who believed that God had ordained natural selection to construct a history of life according to His plans and purposes. Move on another 50 years to the two greatest evolutionists of our generation: G. G. Simpson was a humanist agnostic. Theodosius Dobzhansky a believing Russian Orthodox. Either half my colleagues are enormously stupid, or else the science of Darwinism is fully compatible with conventional religious beliefs—and equally compatible with atheism, thus proving that the two great realms of nature's factuality and the source of human morality do not strongly overlap.[2]

Gould was one of the most celebrated scientists at Harvard and one who had that rare ability to make complex ideas accessible, indeed attractive, to those outside of the scientific community. Such was his prominence in popular culture that he appeared as himself on an episode of *The Simpsons* (joining an exclusive club with Stephen Hawking and Dudley R. Herschbach as scientists to appear on the show). But what is Gould really saying here?

2. Gould, "Impeaching a Self-Appointed Judge," 118.

Gould is acknowledging a fact that should be absolutely self-evident to any impartial observer. There is clearly intellectual material available for the theist and the anti-theist to satisfy their rational side and form the basis of a logical worldview. Some of the greatest thinkers of all time have been fervent atheists, others have been passive agnostics, some have been devout Christians and others still have been committed to different religions. This is a truism not only in science but philosophy, history, sociology, psychology, and any other discipline you care to name. There are two approaches we can take to this evidence. The militant approach is to insist that ideological dissenters from their worldview must be suffering from a delusion. It is of no consequence how many Noble Prizes they have won nor any other accolade or achievement in their field, if they hold a different worldview, they are delusional, foolish, and wrong. Gould's approach contrasts sharply. Although personally an anti-theist, Gould refused to accept this false dichotomy. For him, the evidence was "fully compatible" with both atheism and traditional religious beliefs.

If we take Gould's approach, however, we must accept the immediate philosophical ramifications. If we accept there is intellectual material for both sides, we have to also accept that intellect and rational discourse alone will not provide us with a definitive answer to the question of God or how best we should live. The observable evidence only takes us so far in this debate, and belief or disbelief in God ultimately becomes a matter of faith. For scientists who subscribe to the new atheist school, faith is infinitely more offensive than any other F word in the modern lexicon. Other scientists take a more lucid approach and admit the limits of our knowledge and the central role faith has in all human existence theistic or anti-theistic. The English physicist, Paul Davis, wrote in the *New York Times*:

> Clearly, then, both religion and science are founded on faith—namely, on belief in the existence of something outside the universe, like an unexplained God or an unexplained set of physical laws, maybe even a huge ensemble of unseen universes, too. For that reason, both monotheistic religion and orthodox science fail to provide a complete account of physical existence....
>
> And just as Christians claim that the world depends utterly on God for its existence, while the converse is not the case, so physicists declare a similar asymmetry: the universe is governed by eternal laws (or meta-laws), but the laws are completely impervious to what happens in the universe.[3]

3. Paul Davis, "Taking Science on Faith," *New York Times*, 24 November 2007.

Faith is an integral part of *any* honest worldview. We judge and consider the limited knowledge available to us and then by faith we conclude that what seems true to us is in fact true. When a scientist (or anyone) dismisses all religion as fantasy, claiming their own worldview consists only of facts and evidence, they move with unintended irony into the same realm of unjustified authoritarianism as the religious fundamentalists they so frequently lampoon. As Davis concludes, "until science comes up with a testable theory of the laws of the universe, its claim to be free of faith is manifestly bogus."[4]

Science cannot explain all the mysteries of the universe, however, it can tell us an enormous amount about our world and new discoveries continue to be made. Christianity does itself a major disservice when it rejects scientific consensus based on a particular reading of the Bible. This is an area where Christianity can learn from some of the best atheist thinkers. Removing God and spirituality, the secular tradition is marked by its adoration of learning and the pursuit of knowledge. At the level of human rights and dignity, we are all equal. Atheists, perhaps more than their religious counterparts, are quick to assert, however, that all opinions are not equal and that peer-reviewed academic material produced by experts should be given weight and consideration well above a casual observer or someone with a general interest in a topic. The overwhelming scientific support for evolution by natural selection is a case in point and should not be dismissed lightly on the shaky grounds that it conflicts with some interpretations of the Bible. Biblical literalism is damaging as it presumes the ancient texts to be authoritative on matters of science and history rather than inspired spiritual wisdom. It allows Christianity to be unfairly stereotyped as anti-scientific and anti-intellectual.

The Bible begins with the six-day creation story in the book of Genesis. Following the publication of Darwin's *Origins of Species* in 1859, fierce debate surrounded the nature of the Pentateuch and if it referred to six literal, twenty-four-hour days or not. While all Christian denominations experienced difficulty adapting to modernity, the traditional churches did not endure the same struggle with evolution as faced by Fundamentalists. Inerrancy in the Roman Catholic, Orthodox, and Anglican traditions had a different meaning to the Fundamentalist use of the term. The Bible was only inerrant when interpreted properly by the church. Minor contradictions did not concern early church fathers as the stories were rarely seen

4. Ibid.

as entirely and literally true but rather metaphorical and allegorical revelations. While still guarded and cautious, the traditional churches, and many modern ones, have been largely willing to accept that the earth is billions of years old and that the creation story in Genesis is not a literal, scientific account.

Fundamentalists have reacted far more aggressively to what they see as science encroaching on their faith. In the early twentieth century, the head of the influential World's Christian Fundamentalist Association, John W. Butler, successfully lobbied to have the teaching of evolution criminalized in his home state of Tennessee. In 1925, the famous Scopes trial took place when high school teacher John Scopes voluntarily incriminated himself so that he could challenge the validity of Butler's Act. Although Scopes lost the initial case and was fined $100, he achieved his objective and the case was broadcast to an international audience. H. L. Mencken was one of the loudest voices decrying what he dismissively called the "monkey trial."

The separation of church and state had given way to a powerful Christian lobby desperate to preserve their ascendancy. Mencken wrote as the trial concluded:

> The Scopes trial, from the start, has been carried on in a manner exactly fitted to the anti-evolution law and the simian imbecility under it. There hasn't been the slightest pretense to decorum. The rustic judge, a candidate for re-election, has postured before the yokels like a clown in a ten-cent side show, and almost every word he has uttered has been an undisguised appeal to their prejudices and superstitions. The chief prosecuting attorney, beginning like a competent lawyer and a man of self-respect, ended like a convert at a Billy Sunday revival. It fell to him, finally, to make a clear and astounding statement of the theory of justice prevailing under fundamentalism. What he said, in brief, was that a man accused of infidelity had no rights whatever under Tennessee law....
>
> Let no one mistake it for comedy, farcical though it may be in all its details. It serves notice on the country that Neanderthal man is organizing in these forlorn backwaters of the land, led by a fanatic, rid of sense and devoid of conscience. Tennessee, challenging him too timorously and too late, now sees its courts converted into camp meetings and its Bill of Rights made a mock of by its sworn officers of the law. There are other States that had better look to their arsenals before the Hun is at their gates.[5]

---

5. Joshi, *H. L. Mencken on Religion*, 202.

Mencken's acerbic pen helped polarize the issue with biblical literalism portrayed in stark opposition to science and progress.

Fundamentalism may have won the battle in Tennessee but it eventually lost the war. Following the trial, anti-evolution crusaders were largely unable to make any subsequent victories, and in a public relations sense even Scopes was a shaky victory at best. Despite introducing over forty bills to ban the teaching of evolution in various states around America, the movement gained little traction. With the beginning of the space race in the 1950s, trust in science increased and evolution gained vast acceptance in the academy and in high schools. In response, creation science in the 1960s and intelligent design theories from the 1980s to now have attempted to present creationism as a scientific rather than faith-based alternative to evolution.[6] Funded by the Christian Right, young earth creation apologists have produced hundreds of books, tracts, conferences, and even a Creation Museum to dispute evolution.[7] Some Christians have responded to the broad acceptance of evolution in the education sector by removing their children from public schools. 83 percent of American parents who home school their children cite religious reasons for doing so.[8] Home schooling has seen rapid growth, increasing by 74 percent between 1999 and 2009.[9] This has coincided with the rise of new atheism. Some 1.5 million American students are home schooled and the top home-school textbooks dismiss evolution.

Why is this scientific development so traumatic for some Christians? Why are itinerant young earth apologists dedicating their lives to speaking in small churches and challenging an established orthodoxy that has overwhelming evidentiary support? Why would parents rather home school their children than let trained science teachers use modern text books that reflect the current consensus? Marxist philosopher and atheist Slavoj Žižek offers one explanation. He suggests that humans are capable of wilfully unknowing things that challenge their belief systems or that would cause a behavioral change they are not able or willing to accept. If an average person was to visit an abattoir and witness the slaughter of animals, which

---

6. Lienesch, *In the Beginning*, 198.

7. The Creation Museum is located in Petersburg, Kentucky (www.creationmuseum.org).

8. Dylan Lovan, "Top Home-School Texts Dismiss Evolution for Creationism," *USA Today*, 8 March 2010.

9. Janice Lloyd, "Home Schooling Grows," *USA Today*, 5 January, 2009.

Atheism and Science

even under conditions deemed ethical still contain scenes of fear, violence, and death, it would have an emotional impact. Žižek asks:

> Would the watcher be able to continue going on as usual? Yes, but only if he or she were able to somehow forget—in an act which suspended symbolic efficiency—what has been witnessed. This forgetting entails a gesture of what is called fetishist disavowal: "I know but I don't want to know that I know." I know it but I refuse to fully assume the consequences of this knowledge, so that I can continue acting as if I don't know it.[10]

Unlike abattoirs that are specifically designed to be out of sight and out of mind, modern science and new advancements are disseminated openly in schools and universities, at scientific institutes and conferences, and even in the mainstream media and television. Yet many Fundamentalist Christians manage to cling to fetishist disavowal methods and aggressively reject or tactfully avoid the scientific challenge to their worldview.

Why is it so hard to ask why? This is where Christianity can learn from atheism. Hannah Arendt famously claimed that "thinking is equally dangerous to all creeds."[11] It is dangerous to ask why because the answer might challenge comforting notions. Nevertheless, the question is vital for growth and to understand why we think the way we do. In a study comparing the impact of atheism on children and the family, Christel Manning noted that "the importance of teaching children to 'question everything' was a recurrent theme."[12] This is a laudable trait. The best features of a worldview will always withstand scrutiny and we should have the courage to dismiss the worst. Modern atheism was championed by people who courageously asked why in societies where it was often dangerous to do so.

The work of the Austrian-British philosopher Karl Popper is useful in defining the intellectual space of religion and science. Although a firm agnostic and celebrated figure in the secular tradition, Popper was not against religion (despite some attempts to portray him that way), but rather a critic of blind faith and theistic authoritarianism. He offered the following sober warning, "We all remember how many religious wars were fought for a religion of love and gentleness; how many bodies were burned alive with the genuinely kind intention of saving souls from the eternal fire of hell."[13] This

10. Žižek, *Violence*, 45–46.
11. Villa, *The Cambridge Companion to Hannah Arendt*, 289.
12. Manning, "Atheism, Secularity, the Family and Children," 29.
13. Popper, *Conjectures and Refutations*, 479.

was far from a *carte blanche* attack on religion however. For Popper there was a clear distinction between Christian ethics or using the teachings of Jesus Christ as the basis of a moral framework and the kind of religious fanaticism that holds every dogmatic truth as impervious to criticism regardless of whether it is obnoxious to science, reason, or both. He insisted he was "anything else but an opponent of religion," but spoke out against what he saw as *uncaring* and *unethical* religion, the kind of "Christianity that refuses to carry the cross of being human."[14]

The concept of myth was important to Popper, especially the idea that science arises out of the criticism of myth. In *Conjectures and Refutations*, Popper writes that:

> Thus science must begin with myths, and with the criticism of myths; neither with the collection of observations, nor with the invention of experiments, but with the critical discussion of myths, and of magical techniques and practices. The scientific tradition is distinguished from the pre-scientific tradition in having two layers. Like the latter, it passes on its theories; but it also passes on a critical attitude towards them. The theories are passed on, not as dogmas, but rather with the challenge to discuss them and improve upon them.[15]

The creation account presented in the Bible is an ideal starting point for Popper. The story served several purposes, not least of which was to establish a distinct primordial tradition from the hegemonic Babylonian creation narrative. The essential elements include the introduction of God as the Aristotelian "unmoved mover" who purposely created the universe and, significantly, defined creation as good. Given the vast gulf in scientific knowledge that defines modernity and the ancient culture of the writers of Genesis, Christianity must ask itself whether there are elements of myth in the biblical creation account or whether it is all literally true at a scientific and historical level as well as a theological one.

As a philosopher of science, one of Popper's great contributions to the field is his promotion of empirical falsification at the expense of classical inductivist thinking. For Popper, fallibility was the key element that separated science from religion, the arts, and other pursuits. No amount of positive observations can prove a theory scientifically, but negative observations can *disprove* one, and if a theory can be empirically tested for falsehoods

---

14. Kiesewetter, "Ethical Foundations of Popper's Philosophy," 284.
15. Popper, *Conjectures and Refutations*, 66–67.

then it is scientific. Certain topics cannot be empirically tested, such as the existence of God. These topics are, therefore, not scientific questions by Popper's definition. Some young earth creationists and other anti-evolution Christian scientists invoke Popper claiming that the formation of life as "unique, unrepeatable events of the past that cannot be observed in nature or repeated in the laboratory" is a matter of faith not science.[16] This is specious logic, as we shall see shortly.

In addition, we should note that Popper's falsification method can certainly be called upon to disprove young earth theories. The age of the earth, for example, is not a topic of controversy in the scientific community. It is contested only by fringe groups of young earth creationists who can only reconcile their literal reading of the Bible with an earth that is around 10,000 years old. While the origins of the universe and what, if anything, existed before cannot be scientifically tested (at least not now), physical evidence regarding the age of the earth can be used to easily falsify these young earth claims. We know that the earth is around 4.5 billion years old because we can measure the rate of radioactive chemical decay in rocks. As Christian scientist Francis Collins explains, we know that over time "uranium slowly becomes lead, potassium slowly becomes argon, and the more exotic strontium becomes the rare element called rubidium."[17] All three testing methods have been remarkably consistent in indicating a planet that is 4.5 billion years old with an error margin of just 1 percent.[18] Brent Dalrymple's now canonical text, *The Age of the Earth* describes the scientific basis for dating rocks, minerals, meteorites, and the moon and how each support a very similar age.[19] If young earth creationists refuse to allow their theories to be empirically falsified—and they certainly seem very resistant to empirical evidence against them—then they lose their claims to be offering scientific theories.

If science can be used to debunk young earth creationism, can it also be used to prove evolution by natural selection? Six-day creationists, as we saw above, tend to argue that the origin of life was a unique event, hence unrepeatable, untestable, and unscientific (although they often concurrently

---

16. Notable creationist debaters Isaac Asimov and Duane Gish, for instance, call on Popper to make this claim. See Isaac Asimov and Duane Gish, "The Genesis War: A Debate," *Science Digest*, October 1981, 82.

17. Collins, *The Language of God*, 121.

18. Ibid., 122.

19. Dalrymple, *The Age of the Earth*.

attempt to present scientific evidence for their own views). While Popper did not see evolution as absolutely provable, he strongly disputed the claim that its basis was not scientific. He noted:

> It does appear . . . that some people think that I have denied scientific character to the historical sciences, such as palaeontology, or the history of the evolution of life on Earth; or to say, the history of literature, or of technology, or of science. This is a mistake, and I here wish to affirm that these and other historical sciences have in my opinion scientific character; their hypotheses can in many cases be tested.
>
> It appears as if some people would think that the historical sciences are untestable because they describe unique events. However, the description of unique events can very often be tested by deriving from them testable predictions or retrodictions.[20]

Evolutionary biology does not lend itself to repeatable experiments as none of us can live for millions of years to observe them. That does not mean, however, that the evidence for evolution is not scientific. The earth is replete with clues to its past and evolution has been uniquely successful in tying together this myriad of physical evidence into a satisfying grand narrative for scientists from many diverse fields.

While some ideological opponents of evolution have seized upon the word "theory" in an attempt to undermine its authority—"it's only a theory." However, this strategy usually represents a gross over-simplification of the term and a general ignorance of how it is applied in the scientific community. The ready-made response is that the theory of gravity shares the same prefix. In science, the word "theory" is used to describe the best explanation, drawing on all available data and evidence (as opposed to mathematics, where definitive proof can be provided). To this end, the theory of evolution has near-universal scientific consensus as the most plausible account, drawing in a range of evidences, including not only fossil records but comparative anatomy and embryology, physiology, palaeontology, molecular studies, and genetics also. Catholic theologian, Stephen J. Pope puts it this way, "evolution is the unifying theory of the biological sciences and the indispensible key to understanding the proliferation of life."[21] The renowned geneticist and practicing Orthodox Christian, Theodosius

---

20. Karl Popper. "Evolution," *New Scientist*, 21 August 1980, 611.
21. Pope, *Human Evolution and Christian Ethics*, 81.

Atheism and Science

Dobzhansky, insisted that, "nothing in biology makes sense except in the light of evolution."[22]

The Christian response to evolution has, for the most part, been one of gradual acceptance. Various modes of theistic evolution have become popular, especially in Western churches. Reconciling theology and modern science, the central tenant is that evolution was a process guided by or set in motion by God. Anglicans have largely embraced this view to the point where Rowan Williams, while still Archbishop of Canterbury, stated his opposition to the teaching of creationism as science or a science alternative in schools.[23] He outlined a broad vision of theistic evolution noting that:

> For most of the history of Christianity . . . there's been an awareness that a belief that everything depends on the creative act of God, is quite compatible with a degree of uncertainty or latitude about how precisely that unfolds in creative time. You find someone like St. Augustine, absolutely clear God created everything, he takes Genesis fairly literally. But he then says well, what is it that provides the potentiality of change in the world? Well, hence, we have to think, he says, of—as when developing structures in the world, the seeds of potential in the world that drive processes of change. And some Christians responding to Darwin in the 19th Century said well, that sounds a bit like what St. Augustine said of the seeds of processes.[24]

Williams is quite measured in his language, but the Anglican Communion has also produced a school of theologians who firmly endorse evolution and are critical of traditional Christian interpretations of Scripture. The retired Bishop of Newark, John Shelby Spong, is perhaps the most prominent for his outspoken views that aspects of Christianity have enabled misogyny and homophobia. Together with other notable writers from several denominations, Spong is part of a growing evolutionary spirituality movement.

The Catholic Church has traditionally held a flexible position concerning evolution and has been a relatively quiet player in the debate when compared to Protestantism in general and Evangelicalism in particular. As early as 1950, Pope Pius XII indicated that evolution, while not endorsed by the church, did not contravene any specific doctrine. His encyclical decreed that:

22. Ibid.
23. "Interview: Rowan Williams," *The Guardian*, 21 March 2006.
24. Ibid.

> The Teaching Authority of the Church does not forbid that, in conformity with the present state of human sciences and sacred theology, research and discussions, on the part of men experienced in both fields, take place with regard to the doctrine of evolution, in as far as it inquires into the origin of the human body as coming from pre-existent and living matter—for the Catholic faith obliges us to hold that souls are immediately created by God.[25]

Pope John Paul II went further. Having won some respect in 1993 for officially acquitting Galileo of heresy (360 years after the charge was made), he reengaged with the topic of evolution at the Pontifical Academy of Sciences in 1996. Where Pius XII may have treaded cautiously, perhaps wondering if evolution was a temporary scientific trend, John Paul II readily acknowledged that it had become an established consensus over the previous half century. He stated:

> Today, almost half a century after publication of the encyclical, new knowledge has led to the recognition of the theory of evolution as more than a hypothesis. It is indeed remarkable that this theory has been progressively accepted by researchers, following a series of discoveries in various fields of knowledge. The convergence, neither sought nor fabricated, of the results of work that was conducted independently is in itself a significant argument in favor of the theory.[26]

The response among the various Protestant denominations has been typically diverse, but it would be fair to state that mainline Protestants are inclined to support evolution while Evangelicals, Pentecostals and those in the broader Charismatic movement are more likely to oppose it. The level of opposition in the latter groups, however, is significant and at times fierce. This has far more to do with the framing of the debate than the strength of the creationist argument. Evolution, often inaccurately and derisively referred to as Darwinism, is presented, not as a broad scientific explanation of the development of living organisms, but as a competing theory to Christianity. The *Origin of Species* is presented as a comparable "religious" text to the Bible or Qur'an. Conservative Christians feel compelled to reject evolution, not because it lacks merit—its scientific support is overwhelming—but out of tribal loyalty to their religion.

---

25. Pius XII. "Humani Generis," para 36.
26. Gould, *Leonardo's Mountain of Clams and the Diet of Worms*, 279–80.

Nearly a quarter of Australians in 2009 said they believed the biblical account of human origins over the Darwinian account.[27] A similar 2009 poll found 22 percent of Britons preferred creationism or intelligent design to evolution.[28] In 2012, an Angus Reid poll asked 4,500 people across three countries for their views regarding the origins of human life on earth. Participants could choose between not sure, young earth creationism, or evolution over billions of years. 22 percent of Canadians and 17 percent of Britons believed that "God created human beings in their present form within the last 10,000 years."[29] While a healthy majority of Australians, Britons, and Canadians accept evolution despite a vocal minority of creationists, respondents from the United States were far more skeptical, despite being home to many of the world's leading evolutionary scientists and scientific research universities. 51 percent of Americans chose the young earth creation option with a further 18 percent unsure. Just 30 percent accepted evolution, less than half the response in Britain or Canada. Another 2012 poll, this one organized by Gallup, suggested the figure was lower, but still found a staggering 42 percent of Americans believe that "God created humans in their present form at one time within the last 10,000 years."[30] What is truly extraordinary is that this figure is two points higher than when Gallup first asked the question in 1982.

On the surface it is difficult to comprehend how belief in young earth creationism could be sustained, much less grow, over a thirty year period that saw only increasing scientific consensus and even the acceptance of the Pope. The objections are ideological. A 2014 Associated Press-GfK poll found that many Americans were skeptical, not only about evolution, but also about the age of the earth, the Big Bang, and climate change—all areas where scientists are in overwhelming agreement.[31] Yale's Anthony Leiserowitz suggested the poll highlights "the iron triangle of science, religion and politics."[32] It indicates a firm willingness to place personal beliefs and political persuasion above scientific consensus. To an extent, science will

27. Jacqueline Maley, "God Is Still Tops But Angels Rate Well," *The Age*, 19 December 2009.

28. Riazat Butt, "Half of Britons Do Not Believe in Evolution, Survey Finds," *The Guardian*, 2 February 2009.

29. Canseco, *Creationism and Evolution*, 3.

30. Gallup. "In U.S., 46% Hold Creationist View of Human Origins," line 1.

31. Jennifer Agiesta and Seth Borenstein, "New Poll Reveals Many Americans Express Doubt over Global Warming, Evolution, Big Bang," *Huffington Post*, 21 April 2014.

32. Ibid.

always be politicized, but the public controversy over evolution, in particular, seems entirely needless. It represents a failure on the part of Christianity (more precisely some schools of thought within Christianity) to respect the intellectual boundaries that separate science and religion.

While some schools of thought maintain a suspicion, if not hostility, towards science, thinking Christians have always sought to marry faith and reason in order to gain a better understanding of the world. Before the discoveries of Darwin, the great challenge was to reconcile Aristotelian observational and experimental science with the guiding hand of God. Peter Harrison has written that:

> The combination of Aristotle's final causes and the Christian belief in divine purposes of all natural things gave rise to a new category of literature—physico-theology. This enterprise amounted to a detailed elaboration of the design argument for God's existence, based on the systematic elaboration of divine purposes in the natural world.[33]

Released in 1653, Henry More's *Antidote against Atheism* was particularly significant as it argued against "blind obedience to the Authority of a Church" and in favor of reason and logic to marry the existence of God to scientific discovery.[34] More was heavily influenced by Sir Isaac Newton and his physico-theological ideas in turn would influence Christian thinkers right through to the Victorian era. In a post-Darwinian world, the Christian church is again divided between those who follow the Tertullian example of flight or fight and those who take More's approach of engage and explain.

Tradition tells us that St. Thomas Aquinas once said, *hominem unius libri timeo* (I fear the man of a single book). The Bible is a seminal text of Western civilization and, for Christians, a work of divine inspiration. For all of its wisdom and beauty, however, it is not a work of science and it cannot be logically interpreted as such. Karl Popper's taxonomy of science and non-science is a helpful one and a rational way to define the theoretical realms in which these passionate debates take place. If something, like the age of the earth, can be falsified, tested, and researched, there is no use presenting a literal interpretation of Genesis as a counterpoint. The latter does not possess the falsifiability of the former thus attracting Wolfgang Pauli's aphorism, "not only is it not right, it's not even wrong."[35] Christianity must

---

33. Harrison, *The Bible, Protestantism, and the Rise of Natural Science*, 171.
34. Patrides, *The Cambridge Platonists*, 213.
35. Emam, *Are We There Yet?*, 20.

be willing to accept and embrace the advances of science for, as Pope John Paul II eloquently phrased it, "truth cannot contradict truth."[36] Science and Christianity need not, and should not, be at odds and it is disingenuous to argue that a person must choose one or the other. In a world where education and knowledge is freely available in ways unimaginable only decades ago, Christians must be able to cherish their faith while remaining free to be informed by science. In a digital and interconnected world, Christianity must render unto Caesar the things that are Caesar's and render unto science the things that belong in the laboratory.

36. Alston, *The Scientific Case Against Scientific Creationism*, 32.

7

Atheism and Women

In a recent video called the Atheist Alphabet, comedian Catherine Deveny suggests that atheism has a better track record than religious traditions when it comes to the treatment of women. She comments that:

> Atheists understand what it's like to be a woman. Men have mouths, women are mouthy. Men speak, women are outspoken. Men have opinions, women are opinionated. Men are passionate, women are strident.[1]

Patriarchal hegemony and cultural misogyny is, of course, a historical fact the world over. With the exceptions of New Zealand, South Australia, and a handful of states, it was only in the twentieth century that women secured voting rights in most democracies. Even in the twenty-first century, women in many countries are still excluded from public life through legal or cultural restrictions. Anne Summer's 2012 work, *The Misogyny Factor*, highlights the fact that women continue to face discrimination and prejudice even in Western secular democracies like Australia.[2]

Institutionalized religious sexism is a staple of most atheist debates and books. It is a compelling argument, but it must be remembered that the

---

1. Deveney. "Atheist Alphabet." Online, n.p.
2. Summers, *The Misogyny Factor*.

treatment of women within most religious traditions has generally reflected the social norms of ancient cultures. To this extent, it is hardly surprising that Christianity reflected the cultural patriarchy of its inception and most of its history. Controlling women's lives has been a historic priority for the Christian church. Female clothing, female virginity, female virtue, and female subservience to men are reoccurring biblical themes. The crucial question is whether Christian misogyny comes from social and cultural influences or from the religion itself.

The influence of feminism and the women's movement has seen profound change in the Christian church in a short amount of time. While individual churches have varied, sometimes in the extreme, in terms of accepting a feminist critique of Christianity, the overall change in a few short decades has been remarkable. Gary Gorman notes that:

> The Judeo-Christian tradition, we must remember, has been heavily influenced by a patriarchal system in which the feminist perspective has been read, at best, as a sub-text. . . . Indeed, women's experiences within Christianity have been viewed as other than normative, as external factors that merely supplement the dominant male perspective, which is regarded as the norm.[3]

Today, however, it is usual for many churches to have a husband and wife serve as joint senior pastors. Although still a minority, women have gained access to the power structures of most denominations and exercise leadership at a variety of levels. We are witnessing the development of "a genuine recognition of feminine aspects of religion and of the equal place of women in the church."[4]

The Bible certainly provides ample material for misogyny. In the creation story, it is the woman who is singled out as the cause of humanity's fall. Unlike the version of the story in the Qur'an, where Adam and Eve are equally guilty, the Bible places specific emphasis on the woman being deceived and in turn tempting and leading the man astray. In the biblical account, part of God's gender specific punishment for women is that, "thy desire shall be to thy husband, and he shall rule over thee" (Gen 3:16). The specific blame placed on women is reinforced by St. Paul, at least on a traditional interpretation of his words, who writes, "Adam was not deceived, but the woman being deceived was in the transgression" (1 Tim

---

3. Gorman, "Series Foreword," x.
4. Ibid.

2:14). Influential early-church leader Tertullian followed St. Paul's lead and perpetuated an openly misogynistic interpretation. Of women he wrote:

> And do you not know that you are (each) an Eve? . . . *You* are the devil's gateway: you are the unsealer of that (forbidden) tree: *you* are the first deserter of the divine law: *you* are she who persuaded him whom the devil was not valiant enough to attack. *You* destroyed so easily God's image, man. On account of your desert— that is, death—even the Son of God had to die.[5]

John Roddam Spencer Stanhope's 1877 painting, *Eve Tempted*, typifies this attitude. Cold and indifferent, Eve faces the viewer while offering her ear to a serpent with a grotesque human face. She alone, reaches back to take the forbidden fruit. Gustave Moreau's Eve (1885) tells a similar tale. Seductively positioned with flowing gold hair and a demon on her shoulder, she is both tempted and temptress. Adam is nowhere to be seen.

5. Kvam, Schearing and Ziegler, *Eve and Adam*, 132.

The view of women as corrupters, tempters, and obstacles to holiness has proved resilient. Again drawing on St. Paul there has been a long-standing obsession with female clothing. St. Paul insisted that women should cover their heads stating, "But every woman that prayeth or prophesieth with her head uncovered dishonoureth her head" (1 Cor 11:5). Men, in contrast, did not have to cover up, for man is "the image and glory of God: but the woman is the glory of the man" (1 Cor 11:7). The strict binary sees men as holy and of God, while women are worldly and of the flesh. As a result women are called to obedience and subservience under male leadership. St. Paul writes:

> Let the woman learn in silence with all subjection. But I suffer not a woman to teach, nor to usurp authority over the man, but to be in silence. For Adam was first formed, then Eve (1 Tim 2:11–13).

These verses and others like them have been influential in shaping a Christian patriarchy that saw clearly defined gender roles.

Church history has been profoundly shaped by this gender binary. The second-century theologian St. Clement of Alexandria wrote "every woman should be filled with shame by the thought that she is a woman."[6] Boethius, the sixth-century philosopher and Catholic martyr, claimed "woman is a temple built upon a sewer."[7] At the Council of Mâcon in 586 CE, bishops debated whether women had souls and were fully human (by a slim majority they voted in the affirmative). St. Thomas Aquinas, still heralded by many as the greatest Catholic teacher, argued (following Aristotle) that, relative to man, "woman is defective and misbegotten."[8] The influential Nicene Creed, which is still the standard confession of faith in most traditional churches, controversially states that Christ came to earth "for us men and for our salvation" despite recent calls to remove the word "men."[9] While it was assumed that women were included in the statement, the phraseology is indicative of a general phallocentrism that dominated popular discourses both inside and outside of the church.

The European witch hunts are also significant here as they were fuelled and executed by Christian misogyny. While figures vary, it is generally accepted that at least 45,000 people were killed for the crime of witchcraft in

---

6. Wiley, "Humanae Vitae: Sexual Ethics and the Roman Catholic Church," 109.
7. Walker, *Women Are Defective Males*, 121.
8. Pomerleau, *Twelve Great Philosophers*, 96.
9. Turner, "The Order of Mass: Comforting Words," 69.

early modern Europe, the majority of them women.[10] The gendered violence that took place was justified by the French Pope John XXII who formalized the persecution of witchcraft.[11] Between the fifteenth and seventeenth centuries, a period known as the Burning Times, Christian rhetoric was used to oppress and stigmatize women. A widely distributed and reproduced treatise by German churchman Heinrich Kramer, called the *Malleus Maleficarum* (Hammer of Witches), explained the female propensity to sin and union with the devil. First published in 1487, it charged that women were "imperfect animals" and that "all witchcraft comes from carnal lust, which is in women insatiable."[12] The vilification and persecution of women by organized Christianity is well documented and countless women were humiliated, tortured, and killed as a result. State sponsored physical violence rapidly declined in the post-Enlightenment West (although domestic violence continued and remains today an enduring legacy of shame). Church attempts to control the lives of women, however, have proved more tenacious.

In the West, women have enjoyed legal (if not always social) equality with men for many decades and this is generally reflected in the Christian world too. For all the advances that have been made, however, there is still ample evidence of lingering Christian misogyny and areas where the church could learn from the secular tradition. The work of the French existentialist philosopher Simone de Beauvoir is worthy of consideration. Beauvoir stands tall, even imposingly, at the center of the Western feminist pantheon. She is generally regarded as a key figure in the Western feminist tradition and an influential forerunner to the second wave, post-1968 movement. Her magnum opus, *Le Deuxième Sexe* (The Second Sex), is still relevant, over six decades after its initial publication, for both the public in general and the Christian world in particular.

Beauvoir's precedent in writing *Le Deuxième Sexe* is the basic existential principle that existence precedes essence. This concept is introduced in the first few pages and remains a leitmotif throughout. Femininity or womanhood, she observes, is an abstract notion in society that can be embraced, rejected, thriving, or in danger. She concludes, therefore, that "every female being is not necessarily a woman; to be so considered she must share in

---

10. Levack, *The Witch Hunt in Early Modern Europe*, 23.
11. Grady, *Ten Lies The Church Tells Women*, 134.
12. Kramer and Sprenger, *Malleus Maleficarum*, 47.

that mysterious and threatened reality known as femininity."[13] As womanhood is not a natural state but a social construct it can be critiqued and reinvented. Ultimately Beauvoir suggests that through challenging these social constructs women may "make their escape from the sphere hitherto assigned to them."[14]

Beauvoir's work marked the nascent stage of feminist existentialism. This was certainly seen as radically heterodox to the centuries-old Christian tradition, which asserted that women occupy a natural subsidiary role. Beauvoir also challenged the much more contemporary psychoanalytical theory. Although Sigmund Freud's work emphasized the developmental role of the infantile state as opposed to biologically natural states, he maintains, according to Beauvoir, a phallocentric bias. Beauvoir is particularly incensed at the notion of female castration complex. She asserts that Freud is incorrect when he "assumes that woman feels that she is a mutilated man."[15] Beauvoir's existentialist critique of the Freudian paradigm rejects the notion that woman are sexually inferior to men and asserts they should not be restricted to an inferior societal role.

Beauvoir's feminist existentialism is a powerful intellectual force as it counters several theories that used ideology as the basis of patriarchal *legitimus dominatus*. Leading thinkers of the early church—indeed the Bible itself—supported the notion that men had natural dominion over women. St. Paul's letter to the Ephesians explicitly states that women should "submit" to their husband's authority (Eph 5:22). Joan Kelley notes that even after the Reformation, in the Christian world, the key to "social, religious and political structure—and change—was the principle of male domination."[16] The rhetoric of theological gender politics have dramatically changed. To suggest today that women are defective men, either through religion or pseudo-science, would be seen as a backwards, archaic paradigm. Regardless, the idea that men and women should occupy different spheres has remained stubbornly entrenched in Christian dogma.

Beauvoir's feminist existentialism approach directly challenges the concept of biological essentialism. She draws strongly on the Hegelian notion of "the other" to explain the discriminatory position women occupy in patriarchal society. Hegel suggests that self-transcendence can be achieved

---

13. De Beauvoir, *The Second Sex*, 13.
14. Ibid., 29.
15. Ibid., 73.
16. Wisener, "Luther and Women: The Death of Two Marys," 133.

through acknowledging the other, then contrasting and ultimately recognizing it as the inessential. Beauvoir insists that, hitherto, history has suppressed female transcendence by conceptualizing woman as the other and man as the default subject.

Society had been conditioned to understand that history, philosophy, politics, even actions and ideas, are occupied in the male sphere; "a man never begins by presenting himself as an individual of a certain sex."[17] It is, by contrast, an anomaly of sorts, when a woman makes a contribution to these fields. Beauvoir describes the frustrating position women find themselves in when expressing ideas. A man, she notes, may criticize feminine discourse by claiming, "you think thus and so because you are a woman." If a woman retorts, however, "you think the contrary because you are a man." It is by no means an insult. Beauvoir suggests that the only defence open to women is to claim, "I think thus and so because it is true", as this method negates the concept of the male one and the female other.[18]

The institutionalization of female otherness is a source of immense frustration for Beauvoir. One of the primary benefits of this system is that the one, no matter how lowly and humble, can always take pride as the inherent superior of the other. Beauvoir notes that, "the most mediocre of males feels himself a demigod as compared with woman."[19] This is not to suggest that all men are indifferent to the plight of women, however, "the most sympathetic of men never fully comprehend woman's concrete situation."[20] The one can never truly appreciate the experience of the other.

Beauvoir notes that "no group ever sets itself up as the 'One' without at once setting up the 'Other' over against it."[21] In this regard, women are in the same objectified condition as racial or religious minorities. The critical difference is that women are not a minority. In many ways this makes the task of rejecting the label of the other all the more laborious. Whilst racial and religious groups can draw upon a common history and culture as a means of assuming a subjective constitution, women have been conditioned to identify themselves through the male sphere and thus "lack the concrete means for organising themselves into a unit which can stand face

---

17. Beauvoir, *The Second Sex*, 5.
18. Ibid., 15.
19. Ibid., 24.
20. Ibid., 26.
21. Ibid., 17.

to face with the correlative unit."[22] To a large degree Beauvoir's call was heeded and women did form a stronger collective consciousness, especially during the feminist second wave in the 1960s and 1970s. Although the idea of feminism has been deeply unpopular in many churches, the status of women did undergo enormous change in the same period. Nonetheless, the othering of women remains an issue for the church to consider.

Perhaps the most glaring example of perceived sexism in modern Christianity is the refusal to ordain female priests and ministers in some denominations, thus excluding them from the upper echelons of power. Over half of the myriad of American Protestant denominations allow varying degrees of female leadership, however, this usually involves married women serving jointly with their husbands.[23] Of the traditional churches, the Anglican Communion has been the most progressive, gradually ordaining women priests and bishops since the 1940s. In 2006, Katharine Jefferts Schori was elected Primate of the American Episcopal Church, making her the first woman to lead an Anglican province.[24] The Roman Catholic and Orthodox churches, despite facing a shortage of priests, have remained staunchly opposed to the idea. (Indicating the relative seriousness of the issue to some traditionalists, in 2010 Pope Benedict XVI allowed around fifty Anglican clergy and their congregations to defect to Catholicism in response to moves by the Church of England to allow women bishops.[25])

While the Anglican Church has done more than other traditional churches to deconstruct the female other and accept the spiritual experiences and contributions of women equally with men, official wedding vows used in conservative parishes continue to cause concern. The original vows called on wives to "obey" their husbands, but Australia's Sydney diocese convened a liturgical panel in 2012 with a view to introducing alternative wording. Disappointingly for the progressive wing and liberal lay-members, the panel opted for the nearly identical word "submit" instead. Robert Forsyth, Bishop of South Sydney, defended the decision as not sexist explaining that, "We're happy with this version, where the husband promised to serve his wife, to love his wife, and to protect her and she promises to love and serve and to submit." He added that, "The goal is we want men to

---

22. Ibid., 19.

23. Hess et al., *Sociology*, 392.

24. Utter, *Mainline Christians and U.S. Public Policy*, 166.

25. Jonathan Wynne-Jones, "Catholic Church to Welcome 50 Anglican Clergy," *Telegraph*, 13 November 2010.

give leadership in loving and protecting their wives and women respond to that."[26]

Traditional Christian weddings are steeped in misogyny, as the status of women has historically been little more than chattel property. Notwithstanding the genuine warmth of feeling between men and women that familial and romantic relationships can bring, from a legal perspective, women have been the possession of men, somewhat comparable to cattle. The ownership of women by men is even revealed in the Ten Commandments, which did so much to shape Western morality. The tenth commandment states that, "Thou shalt not covet thy neighbor's house, thou shalt not covet thy neighbor's wife, nor his manservant, nor his maidservant, nor his ox, nor his ass, nor any thing that is thy neighbor's" (Exod 20:17). The fact that women are not prohibited from coveting their neighbors' husbands seems a glaring omission, until you accept the original context—i.e., a patriarchal society. This was not a commandment about lust or fidelity, the seventh commandment addresses that. The tenth commandment says not to covet someone else's property. It is only addressed to *men* because only men owned property. Women were the property (seemingly less valuable than the house but more valuable than an ox).

With women traditionally seen as property, marriage was seen as a property transfer. That is why young male suitors would ask the father's permission to marry his daughter. This is why the bride's family would pay for the wedding and offer a dowry. This is why the father would walk down the aisle and present his daughter to her husband. And this is why the woman was expected to take her husband's family name. Most people are aware that the form and symbolism of traditional wedding services reveal historic patriarchy and many couples choose to reject some or all of these elements. Many women choose to keep their family name, some couples walk down the aisle together, and others write their own vows. Society is not static, however, and there is no reason why a couple cannot maintain traditional elements but interpret them in a new way, through a post-feminist prism. Some men continue to ask for the father's permission as a symbolic gesture of respect, rather than as submission to his authority. The bride's walk down the aisle maintains its popularity, though few conceptualize it today as property changing hands. The form and symbolism of the

---

26. ABC News. "Anglican Church Denies New Wedding Vows are Sexist," lines 25–27.

ceremony itself is a matter of taste. It is the meaning behind the ceremony and how it is understood by those involved that matters.

The marriage itself is far more important than the wedding and Christianity must be seen as a force that empowers women as equals if it seeks to maintain relevance in the modern world. Sadly for many churches, the biological essentialism articulated by St. Paul continues to drive a false gender binary and a necessary othering. His marital instructions in the letter to the Ephesians is still a staple of many Christian weddings across the denominations. He writes:

> Wives, submit yourselves unto your own husbands, as unto the Lord. For the husband is the head of the wife, even as Christ is the head of the church: and he is the savior of the body. Therefore as the church is subject unto Christ, so let the wives be to their own husbands in every thing. Husbands, love your wives, even as Christ also loved the church, and gave himself for it; That he might sanctify and cleanse it with the washing of water by the word, That he might present it to himself a glorious church, not having spot, or wrinkle, or any such thing; but that it should be holy and without blemish. So ought men to love their wives as their own bodies. He that loveth his wife loveth himself.
>
> For no man ever yet hated his own flesh; but nourisheth and cherisheth it, even as the Lord the church: For we are members of his body, of his flesh, and of his bones. For this cause shall a man leave his father and mother, and shall be joined unto his wife, and they two shall be one flesh. This is a great mystery: but I speak concerning Christ and the church. Nevertheless let every one of you in particular so love his wife even as himself; and the wife see that she reverence her husband. (Eph 5:22–33)

This passage has been the topic of much discussion both within the church and among its critics. Taken at face value, it clearly articulates a vision for marriage where the man is the leader or head of the house and the woman serves in a supporting role. This is consistent with the Genesis account, where Eve is created as Adam's "help meet" or helper (Gen 2:18). Various scholars have tried to view these verses through a non-sexist prism and it is not uncommon to hear churches praise the Bible as a handbook of gender equality. If you take a literalist approach, however, and insist that every word and letter is inerrant and authoritative, it is difficult to interpret these verses, and the many others that call on women to submit to male authority, as saying anything other than men and women are not equal;

men are the divinely appointed leaders. The problem is that modernity and Western cultural norms—not to mention reason itself—insists that men, women, and inter-gender people are equal. Many churches respond by contextualizing St. Paul's letters. They can be seen as specific instructions to specific churches as opposed to universal truths. Alternatively, they can be seen as a cultural reflection of the time, not an eternal principle. While convenient, this approach can be accused of cherry picking. Affirming verses are turned into bookmarks and inspirational posters. Uncomfortable verses are explained away or simply ignored. This approach also invites charges of hypocrisy. Many of the denominations that champion the equality of women and have female pastors and leaders still retain their condemnation of homosexuality as a sin. Why do the numerous verses that require women to be silent and submissive not apply in a modern context but the six verses that seem to condemn homosexuality do?

Again, the central issue is how the Bible is read. In Catholicism, the *Magisterium* interprets the Bible for the faithful and articulates the teachings of the church. In 1988 Pope John Paul II released an apostolic letter titled *Mulieris Dignitatem* to address Ephesians 5 and other verses in Genesis that imply male superiority. Reflecting the Western orthodoxy of gender equality, the letter insisted that women were equal to men and that Adam was Eve's help mate just as she was his.[27] The response to Ephesians 5 is even more radical. It argues simply that the language is "profoundly rooted in the customs and religious tradition of the time." The document insists that "The woman cannot become the 'object' of 'domination' and male 'possession.'"[28] This emphasis on equality sits awkwardly with the refusal to ordain women as priests, but it does highlight how malleable the Bible can be.

The place of women in the Christian world has undoubtedly changed for the better over the last half century, reflecting similar changes in broader society. Despite these advances, there is still a long way to go. Just as legal recognition of gender equality does not necessarily translate to social acceptance, sermons and dogma endorsing equal rights cannot immediately unravel an entrenched patriarchal culture. Within Catholicism, the culture has already profoundly changed in the West. It is largely accepted that women can and should perform leadership roles in Mass, such as liturgical readers and Eucharistic ministers. It is beyond question that women

27. John Paul II, "Mulieris Dignitatem."
28. Ibid.

drive and enhance parish life, with some 85 percent of roles that do not require ordination being filled by women.[29] Despite John Paul II insisting that, "the Church has no authority whatsoever to confer priestly ordination on women," Catholicism needs to complete the project of gender equity by allowing women to rise to the top.[30]

Presently excluded, many Catholic women are turning to academic theology. Susan Ross comments that:

> Women theologians work alongside their male colleagues in departments of theology in colleges, universities and seminaries, publish in the same theological journals and, increasingly, hold positions of authority: as chairs of departments, as deans, and as officers of theological societies.[31]

With women continuing to shine in positions of academic and theological leadership at Catholic universities and seminaries, it is a blatant anachronism that they are excluded from the priesthood irrespective of talent and regardless of if they see it as their calling and vocation. Only a few decades ago, the same arguments calling on a thoroughly disproved gender binary railed against the appointment of women to many of the roles they now successfully occupy. It does not take a Nostradamus to predict that women, if ordained, would serve the Catholic Church with distinction, if seen, not as a supporting other to the natural leadership of men, but a full equal with the capacity to carry out priestly duties.

The tenuous argument that Christ himself chose only male apostles can be quickly dismissed. The choice of disciples reflected the cultural norms of the time. Like St. Paul's tacit approval of slavery (Col 3:22, Eph 6:5), it is a reflection of societal tradition. Even within the patriarchy of the time, Christ, if anything, rejected gender taboos by speaking with the Samaritan woman at the well (John 4:10), healing the woman suffering blood loss (Mark 5:24–34), and saving the life of the woman caught in adultery (John 8:7). These may seem innocuous, but at the time it represented a radical challenge to the prevailing gender norms. No theologian would argue that everything in the Bible is an example for life today. The male disciples are a historical fact, but far from a command or an eternal truth.

Another *realpolitik* argument sometimes put forward suggests that Catholicism, as a global church, would greatly destabilize or even schism

---

29. Stewart, *The Catholic Church*, 322
30. John Paul II, "Ordinatio Sacerdotalis."
31. Ross, "Catholic Women Theologians of the Left," 38

on the issue. Women priests may be acceptable in Western nations but other conservative countries in Asia and Africa would never accept it (or so the argument goes). This is where soul searching is needed. Do we really believe in the intrinsic equality of genders or is it merely tokenistic statements to appear relevant? If the Catholic Church is serious about the equality of men and women, leadership is required declaring boldly what is right, rather than what is popular or politically expedient.

The place of women in Christianity and the value placed on their contribution to the vibrancy of the church should be the concern of all. This is one vital front of the acerbic culture wars that divides traditional conservatives and progressive, liberal thinkers. Even within churches that openly declare gender equality, there is often a conflicting, unspoken acceptance of male leadership. Lakewood Church, for instance, boasts the largest congregation in the United States and is officially under the joint leadership of Joel and Victoria Osteen. Nevertheless, the presentation and prioritization by Lakewood's own media department makes it immediately clear who the "real" pastor is. Even on the website, Joel is referred to as the "pastor" whereas Victoria is the "co-pastor."[32] Australia's Hillsong Church places a much greater emphasis on presenting senior pastors Brian and Bobbie Houston as equal leaders, but again the public profile of Brian is significantly higher. It would cause little drama to refer to Brian as the head of Hillsong Church, while few would do the same for Bobbie without the important qualification that she is joint-leader with her husband. In both churches there is a clear male one and a female other. Speaking to a graduate of Hillsong's International Leadership College, I was told that men represent the strength of God while women represent the love and compassion. In order to cling to biblical literalism and reconcile St. Paul's seemingly anti-female equality edicts, a culture of women being considered equal-but-different has emerged. Despite the rhetoric, the end result is, as with many others churches, men dominate the stage and limelight while women contribute behind the scenes.

Beauvoir and other atheist thinkers offer a timely and considered critique to the lingering inequality that is manifested in nearly all Christian denominations. Are women still seen as the other while men are the default subject, the natural leaders in church and home life? There is no question that the writers of the Bible saw gender in terms of a crude binary where men were active, rational, and dominate, compared to women, seen

---

32. Lakewood Church, "Leadership Team."

as passive, emotional, and submissive. Christianity will never be able to empower women in the twenty-first century unless the nexus of patriarchal tradition and the Christian redemptive message is severed. Christians must ask themselves with honesty and boldness if they are allowing the cult of Bibleanity to turn them into apologists for sexism and misogyny. It is a cause of great psychological trauma for many Christians to break the spell of literalism and acknowledge that St. Paul may have been right in the first century while not being right today. Nevertheless, it is an important step to take. Women should not be silent! Any religion that belittles women, that assigns them a separate and inferior sphere of influence, that questions their intelligence and leadership potential, or that curtails their ambitions to be anything other than full equals with men is doomed to fail. Indeed, it deserves to fail.

8

Atheism and the System

FEW IN THE WESTERN world would associate Christianity with radicalism. Having been the dominant religion for so long (for most of Europe since the fall of the Roman Empire and in other Western nations since the time of European colonization) Christianity is generally associated with the establishment, political conservatism, and cultural hegemony. In the case of celebrity pastors and televangelists it even draws connotations of capitalism, greed, and prosperity preaching. This is a far cry from historical Christianity, which began as a fringe Jewish sect, often counter-cultural and "socialist" in nature. Even after the rise of Christianity in Europe, a radical undercurrent remained. The established Catholic Church was forcefully challenged during the Protestant Reformation just as America's Mayflower pilgrims included religious dissenters against the established churches in England and the Netherlands. Christianity has largely lost its willingness to collectively challenge the system in which it operates and critique the negative elements. Perhaps fearful of losing its privileged position in Western culture, modern Christianity has largely become a faithful base for the political Right. Should the church challenge the system even when it favors them? Is this another area when Christianity can learn from the best aspects of the secular tradition?

Karl Marx (1818–83) is a name that still draws intense admiration and loathing well over a century after his death in London. Coauthor of one of

Atheism and the System

the most influential political tomes ever written, *The Communist Manifesto*, his legacy has been anachronistically warped by Cold War politics and a world profoundly different to the one he inhabited in 1848.[1] Marx was certainly an avowed atheist. Perhaps his most famous axioms holds that:

> Religious suffering is, at one and the same time, the expression of real suffering and a protest against real suffering. Religion is the sigh of the oppressed creature, the heart of a heartless world, and the soul of soulless conditions. It is the opium of the people.[2]

Marx was convinced that Christianity was used by the bourgeoisie as a tool of oppression. By promising the toiling proletariat spiritual rewards in the next life, they were encouraged to obediently suffer through existence in the present one. His charge that "true happiness" required "the abolition of religion" is hyperbolic and reveals his personal bias against Christianity.[3] Nonetheless, his critique of religion and his broader call to challenge the system is instructive, not only for atheists, but for the Christian world also.

In his thoughtful work, *Suspicion and Faith: The Religious Uses of Modern Atheism*, Merold Westphal makes the controversial argument that Marx's critique of religion is "deeply biblical, in spite of [his] own unbelief."[4] Drawing on Freud and Nietzsche also, Westphal, a Distinguished Professor of Philosophy at Fordham University, describes the trio as masters of the "hermeneutics of suspicion," a concept of value to those both inside and outside the church.[5] Indeed, he insists that his work "was written more for the church than for the academy."[6] With a refreshingly brave outlook, Westphal asks whether God might even use the enemies of the church for His own purpose. One certainly does not have to be a Marxist to find value and wisdom in his dynamic and iconoclastic works. Even his critique of Christianity should be considered and discussed, not lightly dismissed.

Marx was not concerned necessarily that religion was false but that it was used by the ruling elite to further their own interests and to pacify the working class. Marx reminds his readers that there is an inherent dignity in all humans and that we are all worthy of respect regardless of class. To this

---

1. Marx and Engels, *The Communist Manifesto*.
2. Marx, *Critique of Hegel's "Philosophy Of Right,"* 131.
3. Ibid.
4. Westphal, *Suspicion and Faith*, 12.
5. Ibid., 13.
6. Ibid., xiii.

end he violently rejects what he sees as a project of capitalist dehumanization. In his early writings he claimed that:

> It goes without saying that political economy regards the proletarian, i.e. he who lives without capital and ground rent from labour alone, and from one-sided, abstract labour at that, as nothing more than a worker. It can therefore advance the thesis that, like a horse, he must receive enough to enable him to work. It does not consider him, during the time when he is not working, as a human being.[7]

This is a concept that should resonate with Christian and atheist alike. Human beings are not simply cogs in the machine or beasts of burden yet this is, according to Marx, how the market sees us. The eighteenth-century economist Adam Smith wrote of an invisible hand that would guide market forces. For Marx, left unregulated, the same invisible hand was responsible for applying the manacles to the working class.

Central to Marxist thought is the concept that life has meaning. This is a great similarity with Christianity. Both recognize a value in humanity beyond what they can produce or contribute in an economic sense. Marx makes clear that he does not want people to lose their incentive to work or their motivation to apply innovation and creativity to their labor. Rather, he stresses that this must not be the measure of their inherent value. He writes:

> We by no means intend to abolish this personal appropriation of the products of labour, an appropriation that is made for the maintenance and reproduction of human life, and that leaves no surplus wherewith to command the labour of others. All that we want to do away with is the miserable character of this appropriation, under which the labourer lives merely to increase capital, and is allowed to live only in so far as the interest of the ruling class requires it. In bourgeois society capital is independent and has individuality, while the living person is dependent and has no individuality.[8]

Jesus Christ famously honoured the widow's mite, making clear that his followers should not judge people by their wealth or ability to contribute in a material sense (Luke 21:1–4). Similarly, in the late nineteenth century, Marx popularized Louis Blanc's maxim, "From each according to

---

7. Marx, *Early Writings*, 8.
8. Marx, *Karl Marx: Selected Writings*, 257.

his ability, to each according to his needs."⁹ An ideal society for Marx is one where people have their basic needs looked after, regardless of their ability to pay. Their value is in their humanity, not their ability to produce or accumulate wealth.

Communism is largely seen as a failed and deadly experiment. Shaped by Cold War politics, Christianity in the West has generally seen communists and communism as the enemy; very much a Hegelian other. Nowhere was this more true than the United States, where communists were routinely persecuted and blacklisted under McCarthyism in the 1950s. Consequently, not only communism but the related ideas of socialism and Marxism have been culturally demonized and are still viewed with suspicion even after the fall of the Soviet Union. Yet, the concept of universal healthcare has been embraced in virtually all developed countries outside the USA. It is something of an anomaly that it has received such hostile opposition, particularly from Christians, in the largest Christian nation on earth.

Universal healthcare is based on the principle that all life is valuable and that people have an inherent right to medical attention regardless of their ability to pay. While it is certainly Marxist in origin, it is also compatible with, and in fact should be complemented by, Christianity with its heavy emphasis on helping the sick. When Jesus spoke of the great Judgement Day when God would separate the good from the wicked, the sheep from the goats, he specifically included the example of helping the sick saying, "Inasmuch as ye have done it unto one of the least of these my brethren, ye have done it unto me" (Matt 25:40). And yet, the most vocal opposition to universal healthcare seems to come from the American Religious Right.

Inspired by Marx, the Union of Soviet Socialist Republics was the first country in the world to introduce universal healthcare. Hospitals and clinics, staffed by government salaried doctors, provided care initially to workers in the industrialized cities in the 1920s and 1930s. By 1937, free healthcare was offered to rural areas as well, creating the first universal system.¹⁰ Perhaps wanting to limit the appeal of communism, the United Kingdom and New Zealand followed suit in the 1940s. Democratic nations began adopting the concept gradually over the next four decades. By the 1990s, universal healthcare was well established throughout Europe as well as Australia, Canada, Japan, Taiwan, South Korea, and Israel. Today, several developing countries also have universal healthcare, including Saudi

9. Laidler, *History of Socialism*, 63.
10. Roemer, *National Health Systems of the World: Volume II*, 94.

Arabia, Oman, Costa Rica, Kyrgyzstan, and Cuba. Of the thirty developed nations that comprise the Organization for Economic Cooperation and Development, only Mexico, Turkey, and the United States do not provide universal healthcare.[11]

Why is it that the United States, the richest and most powerful nation in the world, does not offer universal healthcare to protect its most vulnerable citizens? The concept was floated as early as 1912 by Theodore Roosevelt but met stiff opposition. In the 1930s Franklin Roosevelt argued for national healthcare, but, against the backdrop of the Great Depression, pursued social security first. Following World War II, Harry Truman also tried to match the USSR by introducing a national insurance scheme. This was viciously opposed by the American Medical Association, who described it as "socialized medicine." The moniker has proved tenacious. Although Lyndon Johnson was successful in introducing Medicare for the elderly and Medicaid for the poor in 1965, the derisive label of "socialized medicine" was still employed by conservatives in the 1990s and 2000s to oppose universal health plans from Bill Clinton and Barack Obama respectively. Despite having no support from Republicans, in 2010 Obama was successful in extending healthcare coverage to more than 30 million uninsured people with the Patient Protection and Affordable Care Act, derided by opponents as "Obamacare." Immediately challenged, in 2012, the Supreme Court upheld the Act as constitutional.

The startling thing about this intense opposition is that it seems to come largely from conservative Christians, despite the repeated biblical mandate to care for the sick. A national survey suggested that 52 percent of white Evangelical Protestants wanted the Supreme Court to invalidate the Act. Also, 44 percent of white Mainline Protestants wanted the Act stopped, with only 34 percent in support. Of the Tea Party movement, with its strong base in the Religious Right, 71 percent were against the Act. In contrast, only 36 percent of Catholics were against the Act, with 46 percent supportive.[12] Christianity in America is strongly informed by a national commitment to capitalism, consumerism, and choice, and this goes some way to explaining the protracted suspicion around state intervention. Even with the aim of providing affordable healthcare to millions who would oth-

---

11. OECD, "Expensive Health Care is Not Always the Best Health Care, says OECD's Health at a Glance."

12. Public Religion Research Institute, "Americans Divided over the Fate of Health Care Reform."

Atheism and the System

erwise be left vulnerable, an established government health system seems too similar to the established government churches their ancestors fled in Europe. Writing for the *New Yorker*, John Cassidy offers a more individualistic reason for this opposition. He suggests, "Lots of people who don't directly benefit, at least for the moment, because they already have insurance, don't see much in it for them."[13]

Influenced historically by the liberalism of John Locke and the Frontier Thesis articulated by Frederick Jackson Turner, a cult of individualism has been ingrained into the American psyche. The cherished principles of small government, the right to bear arms, the celebration of success, the Wall Street mantra that "Greed is Good," the American Dream itself, are all wedded to the concept of the Protestant work ethic and the requirement that each individual should rise or fall by their deeds. Benjamin Franklin's message that "God helps those who help themselves" has been repeated in pews across the country, but does this ethos leave room for the inherent value in humanity distinct from initiative, drive, and achievement?[14] America does, of course, also have a collectivist tradition, and in the case of healthcare it is perhaps time for American Christians to reconsider their position and traditional allegiance. As the great nineteenth-century poet and essayist Walt Whitman put it, "reexamine all you have been told at school or church or in any book, dismiss whatever insults your own soul."[15]

In Australia, universal healthcare, known as Medicare, was formally introduced by Labor Prime Minister Bob Hawke in 1984. Medicare is funded by the federal government through a levy from which low income earners are exempt. Medicare allows any citizen to see a doctor without charge and the Pharmaceutical Benefits Scheme heavily subsidizes prescription medicine and provides cheap generic alternatives to brand name drugs. Although criticized at times for duplication and inefficiencies, Australia's health system is one of the best in the world. Australian men have the third highest life expectancy of any nation with women sixth highest, according to the World Health Organization in 2014.[16] It seems strange then that the most overtly Christian Australian government in the last half century used its very first budget to dislodge the concept of universal healthcare.

13. John Cassidy, "Obamacare: Where Are We Now?" *New Yorker*, 28 March 2014.
14. Oberg and Stout, *Benjamin Franklin*, 90.
15. Price, *Walt Whitman*, 4.
16. "Australian Men Have Third-Highest Life Expectancy in the World," *The Australian*, 16 May 2014.

Elected in September 2013, the Liberal-National Coalition was led by a devout Christian, Tony Abbott, who trained at one point to enter the Catholic priesthood. Abbott, perhaps more than any other prime minister, incorporated his religion into his politics. Defending his tough border policy stance as opposition leader, he said, "Jesus knew that there was a place for everything and it's not necessarily everyone's place to come to Australia."[17] Critical of the carbon pricing scheme introduced by Australia's first female prime minister, Julia Gillard, he called on the previous government to "repent."[18] While education funding was cut in Abbott's first budget, it is significant that the federal chaplaincy program was continued, but with the proviso that non-religious counsellors be excluded.[19] In Abbott's initial eighteen-man (and one woman) cabinet, Catholics held senior portfolios, including treasurer, finance, trade, communications, education, agriculture, and social services ministers. The remaining ministers belonged to a range of Christian denominations, with none identifying as an atheist.[20]

Given the overtly Christian makeup of the coalition government, it was perhaps surprising that their first budget in May 2014 included a proposed $7 co-payment to see a general practitioner, which would have ended thirty years of free universal healthcare. To prevent people avoiding the payment by going to hospital instead, the government also allowed the states to introduce a $7 fee for emergency visits. The fiscal value of the scheme was immediately questioned with the head of the Australian Medical Association, Brian Owler, warning that, "For some people this co-payment . . . could act as a deterrent, and the eventual effect of that will be that overall medical costs increase rather than decrease."[21] Director of the Deeble Institute for Health Policy Research, Anne-marie Boxall, has suggested the co-payment will "be an unfair burden on people with lower incomes, who also tend to be in poorer health and are most likely to defer

---

17. Michael Harvey, "Even Jesus Christ Would Not Accept Every Asylum-Seeker, says Opposition Leader," *Herald Sun*, 6 April 2010.

18. "Abbott Sets Up Carbon Tax Trigger," *Australian Financial Review*, 16 October 2013.

19. ABC News, "Budget 2014: Funding for Secular Counsellors Cut in School Chaplaincy Program."

20. Jonathan Swan and Lisa Visentin, "Coalition Celebrates a Religious Easter: Eight of 19 Cabinet Members are Catholic," *Sydney Morning Herald*, 20 April 2014.

21. Lenore Taylor, "Tony Abbott Calls Critics of Medicare Co-payment Illogical," *The Guardian*, 27 May 2014.

visits to the GP because of cost."[22] Following a vicious public backlash, plummeting polls, and difficulty passing the legislation through the Senate, the government introduced a modified version in December where GPs would lose $5 from the Medicare rebate but had the option of passing this on to patients. This too failed to receive support, either from the public or Senate. Abbott introduced a second woman to cabinet when Sussan Ley was promoted to minister for health. In March 2015 she declared all co-payment plans were finished, but opponents remained wary that it was an idea Abbott was ideologically committed to.[23]

John Rawls is another secular philosopher who can be instructive when contemplating a topic like universal healthcare. Rawls abandoned orthodox Christianity as an American soldier in World War II but identified as a non-theist, rather than atheist. In his classic 1975 work, *A Theory of Justice*, Rawls looks for moral reasoning that does not rely on God's existence, and supports, among other things, the concept of the veil of ignorance. Put simply, when we argue or take a position on ethical issues like healthcare we, consciously or not, speak from our position as members of a certain race, gender, religion, socio-economic group, and a host of other variables relating to intelligence, ability, and education. Rawls attempts to negate these factors using a thought experiment where "no one knows his place in society, his class position or social status; nor does he know his fortune in the distribution of natural assets and abilities, his intelligence and strength, and the like."[24] Another way to imagine it is; what if you went back before you were born? You did not know if you would be rich or poor, male or female, intelligent or not. If this was the case, if we made decisions from behind a veil of ignorance, what policies would we want implemented? Rawls favors the veil of ignorance method because participants "do not know how the various alternatives will affect their own individual case and they are obliged to evaluate principles solely on the basis of general considerations."[25] Given the percentages and possibilities before entering society, what kind of system would you judge as fair?

---

22. Anne-marie Boxall et. al. "Federal Budget 2014: Health Experts React," *The Conversation*, 13 May 2014.

23. Latika Bourke and Dan Harrison, "Abbott Government Scraps GP Co-payment," *Sydney Morning Herald*, 3 March 2015.

24. Rawls, *A Theory of Justice*, 118.

25. Ibid.

Interestingly, Rawls is borrowing a similar thought experiment employed by the prophet Nathan. In the biblical story, King David steals the wife of one of his soldiers then has the soldier killed. Rather than confront David directly, Nathan takes him behind the veil of ignorance with an allegorical story. The biblical account says:

> And the Lord sent Nathan unto David. And he came unto him, and said unto him, There were two men in one city; the one rich, and the other poor. The rich man had exceeding many flocks and herds: But the poor man had nothing, save one little ewe lamb, which he had bought and nourished up: and it grew up together with him, and with his children; it did eat of his own meat, and drank of his own cup, and lay in his bosom, and was unto him as a daughter. And there came a traveller unto the rich man, and he spared to take of his own flock and of his own herd, to dress for the wayfaring man that was come unto him; but took the poor man's lamb, and dressed it for the man that was come to him. And David's anger was greatly kindled against the man; and he said to Nathan, As the Lord liveth, the man that hath done this thing shall surely die: And he shall restore the lamb fourfold, because he did this thing, and because he had no pity. And Nathan said to David, Thou art the man (2 Sam 12: 1–7a).

David was not considering his immense privilege but was acting according to base self-interest when he took his soldier's wife. Somehow, he justified his initial actions, but the veil of ignorance brought a new perspective. Nathan's technique allowed David to look beyond his own bias and examine the injustice of the situation. What if the roles were reversed?

The veil of ignorance forces us to put aside our personal circumstances. Like the classic board game, *The Game of Life*, we sit back at the table acutely aware of the various possibilities and the element of chance. Statistically, only a precious few will ever be born into great wealth or be intelligent and able enough to gain it. At the other end of the social ladder, a staggering 50 million Americans, one in every six, live in poverty.[26] Even in proudly, though increasingly mythically, egalitarian Australia, more than 2.2 million people, including 600 000 children, live in poverty (roughly one in eight).[27] Further, a Griffith University study has recently suggested "the

---

26. "Record 1 in 6 Americans Living in Poverty: New Census Says the Number of Poor People in the U.S. is 3 Million Higher Than the Official Count," *Daily Mail*, 7 November 2013.

27. ABC News, "1 in 8 Australians Living in Poverty: Report."

poorer, younger and less educated parents are, the more likely babies are to end up at the doctor sick or injured."[28] Given all this, if you were about to be thrust into society, what would your attitude to healthcare be? Would you prefer a universal system where your medical needs are taken care of even if you draw every short straw and are born into the most unfortunate circumstances possible? Or would you take a risk and hope that, if not your economic circumstances, at least your natural faculties would be adequate to let you negotiate a blunt capitalist system?

The politics behind the Medicare co-payment and opposition to Obamacare is nuanced and reactive to a host of competing factors tied to the electoral cycle of both nations. Of significance here is not the inner workings of the political class, but the ideology behind the conservative Christian Right in opposing universal healthcare. In both cases there is a principled objection to people getting something for nothing and a stigmatization of any who take government help as lazy and parasitic. In sum, people should not get something they do not deserve. The glaring irony here is that the entire premise of Christianity is that God's grace, love, and forgiveness is extended to sinners who do not deserve it. For Marx, a religious dimension was not necessary. Shared humanity was reason enough to tend to the sick, so he rallied against a system of stratification that saw people only receive the care they could afford. How much more so for Christians, who have the theological imperative that all are created in God's image and a religious obligation to care for the sick? To some extent the God of the Religious Right has been created in their own image and affixed to the gospel are the new virtues of capitalism, competition, and consumerism. The cultural demonization of Marxism is complete to the point where his congruencies with large sections of the Bible become irrelevant. Indeed, those sections of the Bible become irrelevant also.

Rosa Luxemburg (1871–1919) was a revolutionary socialist and philosopher who fought against class tyranny in turn-of-the-century Germany. Although an atheist, like Marx, Luxemburg insisted she was not against religion but the manipulation of religion by the ruling elite to control the lives of the working class. She condemned the church hierarchy for blindly endorsing the state power structure, writing:

> It is with extraordinary vigour that our clergy fight against the socialists and try by all means to belittle them in the eyes of the

---

28. Tanya Westthorp, "Children from Poor Households More Likely to Get Sick or Injured New Griffith University Research Shows," *Gold Coast Bulletin*, 10 January 2014.

> workers. . . . [T]he priests fulminate against the workers who are on strike or struggle against the government; further, they exhort them to bear poverty and oppression with humility and patience. . . . [T]he clergy storm against the Social Democrats, exhort the workers not to "revolt" against the overlords, but to submit obediently to the oppression of this government.[29]

Luxemburg saw great harm in a form of Christianity that is wedded to the state and uses its influence to encourage political apathy and passivity. In 1897, Congregationalist minister and Christian socialist, Charles M. Sheldon published *In His Steps*, a novel that popularized the now iconic phrase, "what would Jesus do?"[30] Luxemburg asks the same question to her audience.

Historic Christianity and the example of the early church, she argues, should endorse a socialist ideology where the needs of the community outweigh the drive for individual gain. She writes:

> Therefore it would seem as if the clergy ought to lend their help to the Social-Democrats who are trying to enlighten the working people. But that is not enough. We must understand properly the teachings which the Social-Democrats bring to the working class, the hatred of the clergy towards them becomes still less understandable.[31]

As Roland Boer has noted, her message was aimed at the faithful, rather than church leaders. Her message was that "if the Church were true to itself, it would support the workers in their dissatisfaction with and struggles against exploitation. Even if the Church is not on their side in economic matters, it should be."[32] For Marxists like Luxemburg, a Christianity that supports the elite while ignoring the needs of the poor and vulnerable is not genuine. For her, these represent instead the "worshippers of the Golden Calf."[33] Luxemburg's life was cut short when she was brutally murdered and tossed into Berlin's Landwehr Canal. Her voice, however, remains strong and clear, and her message is as relevant as ever for discerning Christian thinkers. She lived and ultimately died for a Marxist ideal that

---

29. Boer, *Criticism of Religion*, 65.
30. Phillips, *Kingdom on Earth*, 130.
31. Boer, *Criticism of Religion*, 63.
32. Ibid.
33. Ibid.

Atheism and the System

should not be anathema to Christians. Indeed, it holds more similarities than differences.

When Marxist theory was appropriated by twentieth-century revolutionaries to create a series of communist states, the results were disastrous. Not for one second should we forget or downplay the horrors and untold millions of cruel deaths suffered in Stalinist Russia, Maoist China, and other places. Without the restraining hand of democracy and regular open and fair elections to hold government to account, the old axiom holds true that absolute power corrupts absolutely. While many died at the hands of communism, it must be remembered also that many gave their lives fighting for it. Be it the Bolsheviks, Viet Cong, Pathet Lao, the MPLA in Angola, Indonesia's PKI, revolutionary Cubans, or many other examples, communists around the world have willingly suffered imprisonment, torture, and death because of a noble dream of a better world. This is the strongest aspect of Marxist thought. It plays to the politics of hope and insists that there is a better way. Where an indifferent market values humanity by its ability to produce capital, Marxism declares that value is inherent *in humanity itself.* Its broad appeal lies in its ability to provide hope to the hopeless.

Throughout the first half of the twentieth century, Marxists spoke with increasing confidence of the crisis of capitalism. Capitalism, they argued, by its very nature, would continue to overproduce and strive to maximize profits by any means necessary. In order for the bourgeois owners of factories and companies to compete, the condition of the working class would be steadily reduced. Marx's immiseration thesis held that eventually the proletariats would have such a miserable existence they would be spurred to revolt and the entire system would be rejected. In his influential 1867 work, *Das Kapital*, Marx wrote that:

> Within the capitalist system all methods for raising the social productivity of labour are put into effect at the cost of the individual worker . . . they transform his life-time into working-time, and drag his wife and child beneath the wheels of the juggernaut of capital. But all methods for the production of surplus-value are at the same time methods of accumulation, and every extension of accumulation becomes, conversely, a means for the development of these methods. It follows therefore that in proportion as capital accumulates, the situation of the worker, be his payment high or low, must grow worse.[34]

---

34. Harvey, *A Companion to Marx's Capital*, 281–82.

Atheism for Christians

Marxism is a broad church and many intellectual schools and variations soon established themselves, especially in the wake of World War I and the Russian Revolution. Regardless, the general assumption that capitalism would inevitably destroy itself remained firm through to the 1960s and in some cases beyond.

By the end of the twentieth century, it became clear to most that capitalism would not end, but would adapt and continue. While some Marxist academics like David Harvey maintain that capitalism is a doomed system, most acknowledge it is tenaciously adaptable and likely to continue. The immiseration thesis proved to be parochial, ignoring the possibility of capitalist owners improving the condition of their workers. Keynesian economics attempted to find a middle ground between laissez faire capitalism and state control. The Marxist critique of capitalism insisted that we cannot rely on the whim of the market without protection for vulnerable people when there is a downturn. This can be disastrous in wealthy nations, let alone poor countries, where economic conditions are almost always bad. Keynes argues that, "The right remedy for the trade cycle is not to be found in abolishing booms and thus keeping us permanently in a semi-slump; but in abolishing slumps and thus keeping us permanently in a quasi-boom."[35] Through regulation and government measures, he argues that the economy can be stabilized and can avoid the extreme booms and busts that causes so much trauma for workers. If the capitalist system is likely to stay, however, what should be the Christian response?

Like Marxists, Christians should have a commitment to social justice and a vested interest in providing hope and encouragement to the poor and vulnerable members of society. Marx wrote that:

> History calls those men the greatest who have ennobled themselves by working for the common good; experience acclaims as happiest the man who has made the greatest number of people happy; religion itself teaches us that the ideal being whom all strive to copy sacrificed himself for the sake of mankind, and who would dare to set at nought such judgments?[36]

It is telling that Marx draws the parallel between Christianity and his own ideas and perhaps even shocking that he describes Jesus Christ as the "ideal being." Ultimately, however, the shared lesson is that humanity has an inherent value and that we should care for the poor and the sick without

---

35. Fikret, *The Global Crisis of 2008 and Keynes's General Theory*, 66.
36. McMahon, *Happiness: A History*, 390.

expecting anything in return. Even within capitalist nations, Christians should draw on Marx and challenge the system where they see inequality and discrimination. Do children from low socio-economic areas have access to decent education, to nutritious food and medical care when they need it? Christians should be at the frontline of the battle for public health and education because they are not only socialist ideas but Christian also. Many Christians may find it anathema to be called a Marxist, but even then they are in good company, as the man himself claimed in response to what he saw as distortions of his work, "If anything is certain, it is that I myself am not a Marxist."[37] Marxism has been twisted and morphed over the years and undeniable horrors have taken place under a red banner. At its core, however, is an ideology that champions the oppressed, that places value on humanity and that plays to the politics of hope. It is a secular tradition the Christian world can certainly learn from.

---

37. Etienne, *The Philosophy of Marx*, 116.

9

Atheism and Clannishness

ALTHOUGH THIS APPLIES FAR more to the new crystal cathedrals than the established churches, Christianity in general is an evangelical religion. Its mission is to win converts and to fill pews. Pentecostal and Evangelical churches in particular, regularly pray for (or "claim," to use popular terminology) entire cities and countries. I often wonder how closely they consider the repercussions of what they ask for. What would happen if they actually did "win" a whole country or many countries? Would society be better if we all held the same uniform belief? The experiment has been played out in numerous settings around the world. Whether it be the Anglican religious hegemony of Elizabethan Britain, the American Puritan settlements of the seventeenth century, Inquisitorial Spain, or various examples in the Islamic world, religious monoculture never produces the utopian society dreamt up by zealous priests and holy people. There will always be dissenters and different points of view. Atheism, at its best, levels the playing field for minorities. We may not all share religious convictions, but we do all share the faculty of reason. Let us then defer to reason when orchestrating public policy and social theory.

Atheism, of course, has its zealots and fanatics, but as a worldview it is less clannish and less concerned with the beliefs of others insofar as they do not impact on others. Even the vociferous champion of atheism, the late

Atheism and Clannishness

Christopher Hitchens, never argued for an atheist society but a pluralistic society where no worldview was given preferential treatment. In a famous tête-à-tête with Douglas Wilson he argued that:

> Religious belief has now become purely optional and cannot be mandated by anything revealed or anything divine. It is one among an infinite number of private "faiths," which do not disturb me in the least as long as its adherents agree to leave me alone.[1]

In an interview with Laura Sheahen he rejected the idea of a secular monoculture as a desirable goal. When asked about the appeal of a world without religion, he replied:

> I ought to wish, oughtn't I, as an atheist, an anti-theist, in fact, that everyone was like her. But somehow, and this may be an irony at my expense, I don't wish that. I rather enjoy the argument. All I'm doing is contributing my little bit to what is humanity's oldest disagreement.[2]

Hitchens was outspoken in his personal rejection of theism, but it is key to note that this was not fuelled by a desire to create a community bound by a common worldview, much less an entire nation or the world.

One of the fiercest arguments within the larger atheism versus theism debate is whether the former constitutes a religion. Atheists reject the notion with tenacity because they do not, by and large, view themselves as a tribe or clan, but a wildly diverse collection of people who simply share one common idea; their non-belief in a God. You will not hear atheists declaring their vision of winning a country for atheism in the way Christians strive to win a country for Christ. Conversion is a fraught subject as people generally hold to their beliefs with enormous conviction. Robert McKim writes that:

> Many people seem positive that their beliefs about religion are right. Often the views of others are thought not only to be wrong but even to be unintelligible or deserving of scorn or ridicule. From the point of view of many members of many traditions, it is unthinkable that they should become a member of another tradition or be anything other than just what they are.[3]

---

1. *Christianity Today.* "Is Christianity Good for the World."
2. Beliefnet, "Worse than Hell: Christopher Hitchens on the Religious Mind."
3. McKim, *Religious Ambiguity and Religious Diversity*, 129–30.

Atheism for Christians

People, of course, do convert or abandon religion, but for the vast majority it is a key part of their identity. While people can and will be organically drawn to Christianity by its merits, it should never be the result of coercion, peer pressure, or violence. The writers of the Bible had no expectation that all people would become Christians, nor did they argue for state promotion. The goal then should not be to create a religious monoculture, but to foster a society where religious diversity is celebrated without detracting from a sense of community.

India's first and longest serving Prime Minister, Jawaharlal Nehru, is a celebrated figure in the secular pantheon. Against a difficult backdrop of religious violence he set an important example by stressing the importance of diversity and religious plurality in a free society. When India won independence from Britain in 1947 it was a culturally diverse nation with many religions and languages. Despite the objections of independence hero, Mahatma Gandhi, the northeast and northwest with a high Muslim population became the separate nation of Pakistan (with East Pakistan becoming the independent nation of Bangladesh in 1971). Pakistan became an Islamic republic, placing religious homogeneity at the heart of the new state. While it is a democracy, the constitution holds that:

> All existing laws shall be brought in conformity with the Injunctions of Islam as laid down in the Holy Quran and Sunnah, in this Part referred to as the Injunctions of Islam, and no law shall be enacted which is repugnant to such Injunctions.[4]

In contrast, Nehru insisted that the new Indian state would be secular, inclusive, and tolerant of other religions. For Nehru, religious differences should not divide a society that shares a common history and culture.

Nehru was named by Ghandi as his successor and is generally regarded as the founder of modern India. With a strong Hindu majority, it would have been easy for Nehru to follow the Pakistani example and draw on common religion to unify the nascent state. Instead, he argued against theocracy and insisted on religious freedom. He noted that:

> We forget that our ancient civilizations, great as they are, were meant for different ages and different conditions. We cannot have today, in an industrial age, an early agrarian economy, such as we had in Vedic times; much less can we have in our country a civilization meant for a desert country more than 1,300 years ago. And many of our traditions and habits and customs, our social

4. Peaslee, *Constitutions of Nations*, 1079.

Atheism and Clannishness

laws, our caste system, the position we give to women, and the dogmas which religion has imposed on us, are the relics of a past, suitable in those far-off days but utterly out of joint with modern conditions.[5]

Nehru faced stiff opposition, but refused to let Hinduism become an official state religion. In the hotly contested Hindu Code Bills, Nehru radically challenged the religious orthodoxy by extending equal property rights to women. As Hermann Kulke and Dietmar Rothermund have noted, "one subject that particularly interested Nehru was the reform of Hindu law, particularly with regard to the rights of Hindu women."[6]

Nehru was an agnostic, but his opposition to theocracy stemmed from a *realpolitik* position. He believed that a religious monoculture was more likely to produce an intolerant society, suspicious and hostile towards those who think differently. He noted with despair, "we see even today that people fight and break each other's heads in the name of religion."[7] The ongoing backdrop of religious violence weighed heavily on Nehru. He claimed:

> It is strange that for the most trivial things, for childish superstition or silly prejudice people take risks and lose their reason in a sea of anger. The vital things, the real things that matter pass unnoticed. Ignorance and bigotry put an end to all rational thought. It is almost useless to argue or convince. Religion is degraded and in its name are done the most shameful things. Indeed religion has become the excuse for many sins. It has little sanctity left and it is trotted out in season and out of season and all argument naturally ends.[8]

Nehru was not arguing that religion was bad in and of itself, only that an official state religion and a society that draws its identity chiefly from that religion leaves itself open to fanaticism.

In the Western world, few nations hold Christianity as an official state religion, yet there remains a strong Christian lobby and, especially in the United States, a sense of religious entitlement. Alexandra Pelosi's 2007 documentary, *Friends of God*, highlights the hundreds of Christian billboards that dot the American landscape. She interviews James Potter who

---

5. Gopal, *Selected Works of Jawaharlal Nehru*, 221.
6. Kulke and Rothermund, *A History of India*, 328.
7. Nehru, *Letters from a Father to his Daughter*, 41.
8. Gopal, *Selected Works of Jawaharlal Nehru*, 211.

is dedicated to building giant roadside crosses at a cost of roughly $25,000 each. The enormous 60 meter crosses in Effingham, Illinois, and Groom, Texas cost far more. While the crosses are on private land, they certainly are public monuments and in some cases popular tourist attractions. They are designed to be seen and, if possible, to convert. Several courthouses have erected monuments listing the biblical Ten Commandments. In 2003, Alabama Chief Justice Roy Moore was dismissed from office after refusing to comply with a federal court order to remove the monument from state land. A CNN-USA Today-Gallup poll suggested that 77 percent of Americans disagreed with the ruling and supported Moore.[9] The Supreme Court is also split on the issue. A framed copy of the Ten Commandments in two Kentucky courthouses were deemed unconstitutional while a 1961-monument in Austin, Texas was allowed to remain owing to its historical significance.[10] In Florida, American Atheists was allowed to erect their own monument next to the Ten Commandments on the courthouse grounds in Starke, while in Oklahoma a Satanist group is attempting to do the same.

Benjamin T. Jones and brother Joshua Jones in Groom, Texas (2015).

9. CNN. "Ten Commandments Monument Moved."
10. Charles Lane. "Court Split over Commandments," *Washington Post*, 28 June 2005.

Atheism and Clannishness

Why is it so important for some Christians to have large public monuments declaring, not only their personal faith, but the faith of the town or city also? The desire to live in a world where only one religious code is visually present has driven some Christians to create a robust theological cocoon where competing worldviews are mentioned only to be dismissed. This was certainly my own experience, growing up inside Sydney's Charismatic Pentecostal movement in the 1980s and 1990s. Along with attending church several times a week, I attended a Christian school, played football in a Christian sports league, spent my holidays at Christian camps, went to Christian conferences, read Christian books, and listened to Christian music (though I did smuggle home a Metallica CD once, landing me in serious trouble). My interest in music deepened and I began learning to play the guitar. Predictably enough, this led to the formation of a Christian band playing at Christian events. I wrote Christian songs and ended up also playing guitar as part of the worship team at Sydney Christian Outreach Centre (now Empower Church) and later Hillsong Church. I was regularly told over the years how I must always be looking to win people for Christ. This was a perplexing challenge for me. Having grown up in such an exclusive environment, I did not really know any non-Christians.

My experience was far from unique and, compared to others, my parents were actually quite liberal. I was largely free to read and watch what I liked and I was supported when I decided to leave my Christian school and enter the public system for my senior years. For most of my friends, leaving the Christian system was unthinkable. Many parents see it as a matter of urgency to raise their children in an exclusively Christian environment and often take on an enormous financial burden to send their children to private Christian schools. For a long time, public schools in the United States generally reflected the Christian hegemony with Bible readings and classroom prayers commonplace. A series of court cases culminating in the landmark Supreme Court ruling, Abington School District v. Schempp (1963), deemed this to be unconstitutional. The most influential American atheist, Madalyn Murray O'Hair, campaigned actively against religion in public schools and for her efforts was described by *Life Magazine* as "the most hated woman in America."[11] In response, many Christian parents have rejected the state system. The Council for American Private Education estimated in 2012 that 30,381, or nearly one quarter of all American

---

11. Le Beau, *The Atheist*, 118–19.

schools, are private, of which the majority are Christian.[12] The independent group Discover Christian Schools quotes A. A. Hodge, stating, "the United States system of national popular education will be the most efficient and wide instrument for the propagation of Atheism which the world has ever seen."[13] They conclude, "the fact remains that public schools are not allowed to give your children the educational experience the Bible demands."[14]

The perception among many Christian parents is not that Christianity is ignored or excluded in public school syllabi, but that secularism is actively promoted. The ongoing battle to introduce intelligent design and other alternatives to evolution into public schools is symptomatic of a general suspicion against any environment that is not explicitly affirming of Christianity. This suspicion extends to tertiary education, where universities, and especially liberal arts colleges, are seen as harbingers of atheism. The successful 2014 Christian film, *God's Not Dead*, certainly played to these fears with a plot that centres on a young freshman resisting the atheistic proselytizing of his philosophy professor. There are over 4,000 degree-granting institutions in the United States and approximately 900 have a religious affiliation. Although less in number, Christian universities and colleges, consciously mixing faith and pedagogy, are available in Great Britain, Canada, Australia, New Zealand, and throughout the Western world. They are becoming an increasingly visible phenomenon throughout Asia and Africa also. From pre-school to primary, secondary, and tertiary studies, Christians can complete their entire education within institutions that explicitly promote their own worldview.

Christian Marxist philosopher and education theorist Paulo Freire would certainly be one to question the legitimacy of this teaching model. In his classic text, *Pedagogies of the Oppressed*, he speaks against what he calls the "banking concept of education."[15] The banking model works on the theory that "knowledge is a gift bestowed by those who consider themselves knowledgeable upon those whom they consider to know nothing."[16] The problem for Freire is that the banking model does not develop deep thinking, social awareness, or foster mutual respect, but encourages intellectual passivity and a classroom of automatons. He writes, "the more stu-

---

12. Council for American Private Education, "Facts and Studies."
13. Discover Christian Schools, "Why Should I Consider Christian Education?"
14. Ibid.
15. Freire, *Pedagogy of the Oppressed*, 72.
16. Ibid.

dents work at storing the deposits entrusted to them, the less they develop the critical consciousness which would result from their intervention in the world as transformers of that world." The popular Christian song by Grammy nominated band *Delirious?* calls for young people to become "history makers."[17] For Freire, this simply cannot happen when students are conditioned to accept the existing power structures without question and obediently internalize the uniform message of their parents, pastors, and teachers.

Of course, it is only natural for parents to want their children to believe what they believe, care about what they care about, and worship as they worship. But there are limits to how far even the strictest parent can control the spirituality of their child. Freire argues that education should not represent a master-slave relationship but a partnership in learning. This involves nourishing free thought and natural curiosity. This means being open to the possibility that the student may be able to show the teachers and parents something new. Freire calls for problem-posing education, where student and teacher alike discuss relevant issues that correspond with the learner's reality and explore potential solutions. He writes:

> In problem-posing education, people develop their power to perceive critically *the way they exist* in the world *with which* and *in which* they find themselves; they come to see the world not as a static reality, but as a reality in process, in transformation.[18]

Presenting a religious monoculture to children may seem like an ideal way of protecting them from evil influences, but too often the immediate effect is to inoculate them from critical thinking and develop a deep clannishness. The long-term impact is often underdeveloped socialization and great trauma and difficulty adapting to a wider world with a myriad of people and ideas. Ultimately, Christian parents should want their children to embrace the faith because they see the benefit, the beauty, and the logic in it, not because it is the only worldview they were ever exposed to.

For many, Christianity is a tribal, ideological bunker; a defensive shield of protection against the arrows of temptation fired from an outside force known simply and pejoratively as "the world." The desire to live in an exclusively Christian environment has given birth to a lucrative Christian market where religious alternatives to virtually anything a person could

---

17. Delirious?, *King of Fools*.
18. Freire, *Pedagogy of the Oppressed*, 83.

want or need are offered. Christian children can grow up in Christian schools, playing with Christian toys, enjoying Christian books, music, shows, and camps. They can even visit the Holy Land Experience, a Christian theme park to challenge Disney World in Orlando, Florida. For adults, there are Christian cook books, weight loss programs, business seminars, putt-putt golf venues, professional wrestling organizations, magazines, television shows, movies, holiday packages, sports teams, and social clubs of every persuasion. Is this willing disconnect from broader society and the marketplace of ideas healthy or helpful?

In his famous poem, *A Charm*, Rudyard Kipling writes of the need to "cleanse and purify" the "webbed and inward-turning eye."[19] Too often Christians are so afraid that they or their children might backslide or have their faith compromised that they create an impenetrable religious bubble where they see out their existence safe from exposure to new ideas. By seeing everything outside of one specific branch of Christianity as a potential stumbling block, the opportunity to grow and develop is often ignored. This is one of the great strengths of secular thinking. *At its best*, atheism will always entertain and discuss new ideas because there is no tribal loyalty and no specific tradition to defend. Nehru said that:

> Organised religion, allying itself to theology and often more concerned with vested interests than with things of the spirit, encourages a temper which is the very opposite to that of science. It produces narrowness and intolerance, credulity and superstition, emotionalism and irrationalism. It tends to close and limit the mind of man, and to produce a temper of a dependent, unfree person.[20]

Of course, it does not have to be this way. Christianity can be, and so often is, inviting, open, and inclusive. It is natural to hold your worldview and religious outlook close to your heart, just as all parents want to impart their knowledge and wisdom onto their children. What must be guarded against is an attitude of religious exceptionalism and a desire to silence all competing voices, especially in public space.

The formal study of philosophy can seem daunting to those uninitiated in its art. At an academic level especially, the esoteric language and complex syllogisms often serve to exclude rather than invite newcomers to the table of conversation. This is where popular philosophers like Alain de

---

19. Kipling, *The Collected Poems of Rudyard Kipling*, 521.
20. Nehru, *The Discovery of India*, 513.

Botton serve such an important function in making philosophy accessible. Secular philosopher Simon Blackburn is also of this mold and his work, *Think*, encourages readers to view philosophy, not as an idle collection of abstractions but as a practical tool for deconstructing arguments and critically assessing claims and problems.[21] In a lecture titled *Why Bother to Think*, he argues that:

> People who have cut their teeth on philosophical problems of rationality, knowledge, perception, free will, and other minds are well placed to think better about problems of evidence, decision making, responsibility, and ethics that life throws up.[22]

Critical thinking is not possible in a state of cultural inertia. While it is tempting to limit yourself to ideas and concepts that reaffirm your default position, we are so much the richer when we move beyond tribal loyalties and examine honestly the range of philosophical views out there, taking from each what wisdom we may.

Humans are naturally tribal creatures and we will always gravitate towards others who share similar features and ideas to ourselves. Christianity is a personal belief, but it is also a cultural sign and a key aspect of a believer's identity. Christians should be mindful of Nehru's example, however, especially at the level of a state. It does not strengthen a nation when one religion is privileged, even if that is the religion of the majority. Rather the opposite is true. A state religion only serves to alienate minorities and impair social cohesion. At a personal level also, Christians should be wary of creating an insular world for themselves where other ideas are kept strictly at the periphery. Prominent atheist author Ayaan Hirsi Ali writes that "without doubts, without a standpoint reached through questioning, human beings can't acquire knowledge."[23] Christianity has nothing to fear from competing worldviews as the best aspects will always withstand scrutiny. The aspects that require clannishness and a myopic outlook to survive are not worth preserving.

---

21. Blackburn, *Think*.

22. Peter Edidin, "Ideas & Trends: Philosophy in Hiding; I Have Tenure, Therefore I Am," *New York Times*, 28 January 2001.

23. Ali, *The Caged Virgin*, 20.

10

Atheism and the Politics of Fear

On 3 October 2014, the Christian blockbuster *Left Behind*, starring Nicolas Cage, was released at over 1800 screens across North America. With four times the original budget ($16 million compared to $4 million), it was a major reworking of the 2000 release, *Left Behind: The Movie*. Both films, based on the best-selling novel series by Tim LaHaye and Jerry B. Jenkins, take a premillennial Christian perspective and focus on the dramatic elements of biblical prophecy, including the rapture, tribulation, and end times. In both movies, Christians suddenly disappear all over the world and are raptured into heaven while non-Christians are left behind to face seven years of war and suffering. In the 2000 version, starring Kirk Cameron, the United Nations is presented as a maleficent one-world government controlled by the Antichrist. Those who accept Christianity after the rapture and choose to endure increasing persecution rather than join the Antichrist, can yet be saved. If the plot is at times nebulous and even contradictory, the message is crystal clear; accept Jesus Christ now or be left behind.

The Cameron version received generally negative reviews, with a score of just 16 percent on popular film review site, Rotten Tomatoes.[1] *New York*

---

1. Accurate as of 24 July 2014. http://www.rottentomatoes.com/m/left_behind_the_movie/.

Times reviewer Stephen Holden typified many responses when he wrote, "as for basic credibility, 'Left Behind' proudly belongs to the don't ask, don't explain, connect no dots school of storytelling."[2] *Left Behind* was certainly a source of amusement for some. It was even parodied by *The Simpsons*. In the episode, "Thank God, It's Doomsday", Homer is stuck by fear after watching an obvious pastiche titled "Left Below" and becomes obsessed with numerology in an attempt to predict the date of the rapture.[3] For the movie's real target audience, however, Christians and those with some Christian background, the themes are nothing to laugh about.

The Nicolas Cage version has received near universal scorn. Rotten Tomatoes gave it a score of just 2 percent.[4] The *Washington Post*'s Michael O'Sullivan was consistent with most mainstream reviews when he wrote, "The film is amateurish on almost every level."[5] The *Toronto Sun* suggested Oscar winner Cage was only interested in the money when he signed on. Liz Braun notes, "Pollsters can tell you that 41% of adult Americans believe in the Rapture and all the accompanying disaster the bible predicts. . . . If audience potential for *Left Behind* is any indication, [Cage is] laughing (maniacally, probably) all the way to the bank."[6]

In a thoughtful piece for *Christianity Today*, Jackson Cuidon argues that "*Left Behind* is not a Christian Movie, whatever 'Christian Movie' could even possibly mean," but an attempt to tap into a lucrative but insecure market, desperate for mainstream validation. He writes:

> You know how you feel when you hear the name of your hometown, and your ears perk up, and you want to talk about it? . . . This isn't a bad thing. What's a bad thing is that Hollywood producers now know that American Christians feel that way about their faith—that Christians so desperately want to participate in the mainstream[,] . . . that Christians just want to feel identified without having to carve out little alcoves or niche markets that exist alongside the Big Boys. . . . [The producers] want churches to

---

2. Stephen Holden, "*Left Behind: the Movie* (2000) Film Review; A Biblically Inspired Tale about Dying and Surviving," *New York Times*, 2 February 2001.

3. The Simpsons. "Thank God, It's Doomsday," Season 16, Episode 19, 2005.

4. Accurate as of 1 March 2015. http://www.rottentomatoes.com/m/left_behind_2014/.

5. Michael O'Sullivan, "Left Behind Movie Review: Reboot Costs More, Adds Nicolas Cage to Amateurish Mix," *Washington Post*, 3 October 2014.

6. Liz Braun, "Left Behind Review: Nicolas Cage Bible Movie is God-Awful," *Toronto Sun*, 3 October 2014.

book whole theatres and take their congregations, want it to be a Youth Group event, want magazines like this one to publish Discussion Questions at the end of their reviews—want the system to churn away, all the while netting them cash, without ever having to have cared a *shred* about actual Christian belief.[7]

Whether the film was designed to make money or promote the Christian message (or both), its content is the most recent in a long history of end-times shock material. Appealing to humanity's inherent fear of death and fear of the unknown, an established genre has asked millions of people if they know how they will spend eternity.

Cameron's *Left Behind* eventually became part of a trilogy of films and, despite the negative reviews, it is likely Cage's commercially profitable adaptation will follow suit. Although these films are based on the books by LaHaye and Jenkins, the whole series owes its inspiration to a similar tetralogy from the 1970s and 1980s produced by Russell S. Doughten. The most influential of these, *A Thief in the Night* (1972), was the first to inject a Christian film with elements of horror and science fiction. Reportedly seen by over 300 million people, it was, "a film that wrecked havoc on the sleep of millions of souls in America and around the world."[8] Like *Left Behind*, the film's premise is the rapture of all "real" Christians. The film's star, Patty, wakes to find her husband has gone and even though she considered herself a Christian because she occasionally went to church and read the Bible, she was left to suffer the tribulation. The Antichrist rises to power and all citizens must have 0110 tattooed three times on their forehead or hand in order to use money and purchase food. The tattoo is binary code of 666, the supposed number of the beast (Rev 13:18).[9] Those who accept Christianity after the rapture face persecution and eventually death, but if they stand fast and refuse the mark, they too go to heaven. Although made with a general intention of spreading the gospel, the movie presented a specific challenge to the Christian world. Are you a "real" Christian or merely a cultural Christian? Would you be raptured to heaven or left to suffer the torments of the great tribulation? What about your children and loved ones?

A Thief in the Night was also one of the first movies to include elements from the hippy influenced Jesus Movement and the burgeoning Christian

---

7. Cuidon, "Left Behind: Not a 'Christian Movie.' Not Even Close," para 1–2.

8. Anderson. "The Original Left Behind," lines 1–2.

9. As was mentioned in an earlier chapter, there is some debate if the number was 616 or 666.

Rock scene.[10] The film prominently used Larry Norman's dispensational song, *I Wish We'd All Been Ready*, inspired by Matthew 24:36–44. A young Christian band sing over a menacing drum beat that the rapture will come suddenly and all who are not ready will be doomed to suffer.

Again, this may seem like an empty threat or even comically melodramatic, but for those raised in the Christian world especially, the prospect of being left behind to face prophetic torments is genuinely terrifying. As a nine-year-old child growing up in the Charismatic Pentecostal movement, I remember getting lost from my family at the local swimming pool. My first reaction was horror and despair as I presumed the rapture had happened and I had been left behind. Contemplating a new life alone, I earnestly repented for my sins (whatever they were, as a quiet and generally well-behaved child) and hoped I might be spared the tribulation, before eventually spotting my parents. Growing up, I frequently re-prayed a salvation prayer, desperate to avoid Patty's fate.

These end-time stories have a long pedigree dating back to the beginning of the Fundamentalist movement in the United States. In 1905 Joseph Birkbeck Burroughs released the most influential of the early prophesy novels, *Titan, Son of Saturn: The Coming World Emperor: The Story of the Other Christ*. Although *Titan* contained many highly unorthodox ideas, especially the idea that Satan was originally intended to be the Messiah, the end times genre proved extremely popular. From 1914, the book included pastoral commendations, including one from leading Evangelical, James M. Gray, who would contribute to the influential essay series that birthed the Fundamentalist movement, *The Fundamentals*.[11] By 1917, *Titan* was in its tenth edition having surpassed ten thousand sales.[12] Joshua Hill's 1910 work, *The Judgement Day: A Story of the Seven Years of the Great Tribulation*, further established the dispensational prophesy genre, as did Sydney Watson's trilogy, *Scarlet and Purple* (1913), *Mark of the Beast* (1915), and *Twinkling of an Eye* (1916). As Richard Kyle notes, "all of these early novels were written as the dominance of the old white Anglo-Saxon world was coming to an end and revealed the anxieties of this cultural group."[13]

The end-times genre, both in literature and film, responds to fear and inspires fear. The early novels often revealed a fear of communism,

---

10. Donald W. Thompson, *A Thief in the Night*. Mark IV Pictures, 1972.
11. Gribben, *Writing the Rapture*, 33.
12. Ibid.
13. Kyle, *Apocalyptic Fever*, 193.

fascism, Judaism, Catholicism, and liberalism more generally. Others were flavored by the experience of the world wars, the Great Depression, and the Scopes Trial. Forest Lonmar Oilar's 1937 work, *Be Thou Prepared for Jesus is Coming*, borders on Luddism, with an inherent distrust of modernism. Written as Europe desperately resisted Nazi domination in 1941, Dayton A. Manker's *They That Remain: A Story of the End Times* (1941) painted a dystopian vision of a post-rapture world, where Jewish-inspired communism dominated society. He posed the question that would prove extremely popular for future end-times works; what would happen to those left behind? Against the backdrop of the Cold War and with the establishment of the state of Israel seen as the fulfillment of biblical prophecy, the end-times genre continued to gain traction. Hal Lindsay's 1970 best seller, *The Late, Great Planet Earth*, was particularly significant. Convinced that contemporary events, such as rising levels of skin cancer and the menace of Brazilian killer bees, combined with tensions in world politics and a general decline in morality proved the imminent coming of the Antichrist and end of the world, Lindsay's book served as a dramatic warning to, in the popular parlance, "turn of burn." Turned into a Hollywood feature in 1978, the book would sell over 20 million copies by 1990, revitalizing the end-times genre and further popularizing dispensational eschatology.

In the 1970s and 1980s a growing interest and awareness in witchcraft, astrology, the occult, and neo-paganism was a cause for great alarm in the Christian world and further proof for end-times writers that the end was indeed near. The success and enormous cultural impact of *The Exorcist* (1973) and its sequels in 1977 and 1990 served to underline the appetite for supernatural themes. Constance E. Cumbey's 1985 work, *The Hidden Dangers of the Rainbow: The New Age Movement and Our Coming Age of Barbarism*, turned the focus to the spiritual battle and the need for protection against demonic attack. Frank Peretti's highly successful novels continued this trend. *This Present Darkness* (1986) and *Piercing the Darkness* (1989) combined elements of suspense and horror, earning Peretti the nickname "the Stephen King of evangelical culture."[14] Although his works do not deal with the rapture, they are concerned with the interactions of angels and demons and the human world. Both novels present the idea of a battle between good and evil and fit in with the broader notion of a coming apocalypse. Again, fear is a driving force. Not only is there the fear of being left behind, but a new fear also of demonic possession and spiritual attack.

14. Gribben, *Writing the Rapture*, 111.

Following the fall of the Soviet Union, the politics of fear continued to inform Christian pop culture. The fear of communism was replaced with a general fear of encroaching secularism and lost morality. The *Left Behind* books began in 1995 with *A Novel of the Earth's Last Days* and would include sixteen titles by 2007. The series has sold over 65 million copies in thirty languages and has spawned a range of additional products, including graphic novels, audio dramatizations, video games, television series, and, of course, the film adaptations. Perhaps disturbingly, there is also a children's version, *Left Behind: The Kids*, to ensure that even the very young can know of the coming tribulation of those who do not accept Christ. The *Left Behind* series also introduces a fear of globalization, with the United Nations depicted as the Antichrist's tool for achieving a one-world government.

LaHaye and Jenkins openly discuss the use of fear in their work. They argue that the dread of being left behind after the rapture "may be the greatest evangelistic tool in human history."[15] The politics of fear have been employed since the birth of the end-times genre, but does this present Christianity as a positive influence that can enrich an individual's life and their world around them or is it a modern adaptation of the Spanish Inquisition? Are people being coerced into choosing Christianity simply to avoid some terrible pain? William Powell Tuck, who critiques the theology behind the *Left Behind* books writes:

> When you think about it, what person would not want to respond to Christ when almost every day terrible plagues are affecting people that cause them pain, suffering, confusion, dread and awesome fear? Almost anyone would to avoid any more suffering. But this raises [a] concern[:] . . . what does this say about the "character" of God? It does not depict a God of love but one who wants to chastise, punish and make humanity suffer to respond to him. This picture reminds me of the pagan gods of Rome and Greece, not the God of love and grace that Jesus Christ revealed.[16]

The same can be said of *A Thief in the Night*. Popular Christian children's author, Dean A. Anderson, acknowledges that the film "truly did inspire fear in many who woke up in an empty house, wondering if they had been left behind."[17] Yet he concludes that "such urgency and intent

---

15. Tuck, *The Left Behind Fantasy*, 113.
16. Ibid., 114.
17. Anderson, "The Original Left Behind," lines 56–58.

to ultimately bring people to Christ will never go out of fashion."[18] Well intentioned as he may be, Anderson is essentially giving an apologia for deliberately terrifying adults and even children, so long as it is done to promote Christianity. The ends, or in this case the end times, justify the means.

Thomas Hobbes was a seventeenth-century English thinker and a major figure in the Western philosophical tradition. He is best known for *Leviathan*, his 1651 political *tour de force*, which established social contract theory. Although he refers to God in his works, there is a popular school of thought that suggests Hobbes was an atheist who professed theism to preserve his career, if not his life. It is clear in any case that Hobbes did not subscribe to orthodox Christianity. In *Leviathan* he critiques the way Christianity it taught and practiced. He writes:

> And this Feare of things invisible, is the naturall Seed of that, which every one in himself calleth Religion; and in them that worship, or feare that Power otherwise than they do, Superstition.[19]

Hobbes is outlining the same objection critics of *Left Behind* might raise. Christianity must be merit-based not fear-based if it is to have a legitimate claim on cultural space. Relying on a celestial bully winning converts through fear only opens Christianity up to the worst criticisms of the new atheists. And yet, as if through defensive reflex, fear seems to dominate the discourse.

The phenomenon of Evangelical Hell Houses is another arena where the politics of fear are used as the primary weapon to win converts to Christianity. Growing in popularity in the 1980s and 1990s, the Hell Houses are Christian versions of Halloween-themed haunted houses. Sometimes attributed to Evangelical leader, Jerry Falwell, a typical experience involves lavish costumes, sets, and high-impact drama. Gregory S. Jackson describes the process:

> Inside the hell house, a docent in demonic guise—wearing a black gown and a skull mask, and carrying a trident—guides visitors through seven or eight chambers, each exhibiting a graphic, disturbing vignette of what many conservative evangelicals consider the most threatening forms of immorality that entice the young today. Each room reveals a different sin, with special focus not

---

18. Ibid.
19. Hobbes, *Leviathan*, 75.

only on the act itself, but also on its consequences both in the temporal world and in eternity.[20]

Although each Hell House is unique and reflects the priorities, concerns, and budget of the church or youth group involved, there is a reasonably standard format and even Hell House kits that can be purchased. There is almost always a bloody and graphic portrayal of an abortion—usually the result of a rape at a drunken party, where the young girl in question tried drugs. A gay teenager is often portrayed in another room, weeping and covered in skin lesions; the demonic host tells the audience that he is dying of AIDS as a result of his sinful lifestyle. Alcohol and drug use, domestic violence, school shootings, fornication, masturbation, pornography, and suicide are common themes also.

The rising popularity of these gruesome live performances led to the 2002 documentary *Hell House*. Focusing on a Hell House set up by Trinity Church in Cedar Hill, Texas, the film explores the motives and logic of the organizers and some of the responses from the audience. Trinity Church put on a grand production with a total audience of some 13,000 people. The film opens with an organizer explaining the *raison d'être* behind the intentionally shocking and scary nature of the Hell House. He says, "I wish you didn't have to see the things you're going to see," but insists if he did not their blood would be on his hands.[21] The film includes disgruntled audience members who object to the perceived homophobia, with one stating, "this is why people are so turned off to the Christian message."[22] For the most part, the audience response is the intended one of shock and alarm.

The climax of the Trinity Church production sees one young man who gave his life to Christ on his deathbed enter the gates into heaven while several other characters are dragged away. In hell, a teenage boy who believed the "lie" that he was born gay and a teenage girl who committed suicide as a result of her abusive family life are shown being tortured for eternity by demons. Finally, the audience is led into a room where a preacher invites any who are not sure if they are going to heaven or hell to pray with their counsellors. Incredibly, he says they have no interest in "scare tactics," but the claim is somewhat disingenuous considering the ordeal the audience has just been through. The counsellor's room is shown full of people, including children in pyjamas, several of them crying as a

20. Jackson, *The Word and Its Witness*, 38.
21. Ratliff, *Hell House*.
22. Ibid.

result of their experience. The first well-known Hell House organized by Falwell in 1972 was promoted as "Scaremare" and it is clear that fright is also a key ingredient for Trinity Church. The Hell House production is a cultural descendent of Dante's *Inferno* with its intimate description of the punishment of sinners. The film finishes with the claim Trinity Church has seen 15,000 people convert or recommit to Christianity over the ten years that Hell House has operated. It has to be wondered, what was the nature of such decisions. The Hell House genre channels the spirit of the hellfire and judgment New England preacher, Solomon Stoddard. In his classic Puritan text, *A Guide to Christ*, he wrote, "if men be thoroughly scared, they will dread doing what wounds their consciences; *fear of Hell* will make men *afraid of sin.*"[23]

Often unintentionally, sometimes, as we have seen, quite deliberately, the politics of fear have a long tradition within Christianity. In *Religion of Fear*, Jason C. Bivins explores the pervasive nature of "fear regimes" that are particularly conspicuous in Evangelical and Fundamentalist circles.[24] He suggests that the decline of Christian America and a creeping secularization has fostered a new manifestation of religious fear revealed in Evangelical pop culture. Carlos R. Bovell has suggested the present Evangelical climate is "characterized by fear," making it difficult to challenge or explore theological issues such an inerrancy.[25] The politics of fear is another area where atheistic thinking can be instructive. At its best, it is a worldview that calls for critical thinking and sound evaluation, rather than emotional manipulation.

The word "secularist" was coined and popularized by British social missionary and newspaper editor George Jacob Holyoake (1817–1906). Following a public lecture in Cheltenham in 1842, he became the last man to be charged and convicted of blasphemy in England, resulting in a six-month sentence. Holyoake was a household name in secular and free thinking circles. Against the backdrop of Darwinian science, he urged his supporters to follow evidence and their own natural curiosity without fear of condemnation or ridicule. In his 1896 work, *Origin and Nature of Secularism*, he outlines the importance of open debate and discourse, free from the politics of fear and coercion. He writes:

---

23. Jackson, *The Word and Its Witness*, 37.
24. Bivins, *Religion of Fear*.
25. Bovell, *Rehabilitating Inerrancy in a Culture of Fear*, 22.

Atheism and the Politics of Fear

> Free thought means fearless thought. It is not deterred by legal penalties, nor by spiritual consequences. Dissent from the Bible does not alarm the true investigator, who takes truth for authority not authority for truth. The thinker who is really free, is independent; he is under no dread; he yields to no menace; he is not dismayed by law, nor custom, nor pulpits, nor society—whose opinion appalls so many. He who has the manly passion of free thought, has no fear of anything, save the fear of error.[26]

Contemporary American free-thought leader and orator Col. Robert G. Ingersoll said in a tribute to Holyoake:

> There is not in this world a nobler, braver man. In England he has done more for the great cause of intellectual liberty than any other man of this generation. He has attacked all abuses, all tyranny and all forms of hypocrisy. His weapons have been reason, logic, facts, kindness, and above all, example.[27]

Following his death, one of America's few free-thought newspapers, the *Blue Grass Blade* of Lexington, Kentucky, honored Holyoake as the "Father of Secularism."[28]

Holyoake's call to be free from fear had a deep impact on the great Welsh philosopher Bertrand Russell, one of the most celebrated minds in the secular pantheon. In a famous 1927 speech to the National Secular Society in London, he outlined the nexus he saw between religion, Christianity in particular, and the politics of fear. He said:

> Religion is based, I think, primarily and mainly on fear. It is partly the terror of the unknown and partly, as I have said, the wish to feel that you have a kind of elder brother who will stand by you in all your troubles and disputes. Fear is the basis of the whole thing—fear of the mysterious, fear of defeat, fear of death. Fear is the parent of cruelty, and therefore it is no wonder if cruelty and religion have gone hand in hand.[29]

For Russell, fear itself was an unavoidable symptom of religion rather than a manifestation in some circumstances.[30] This does not have to be the case and, indeed, often is not.

26. Barker, *The Good Atheist*, 164.
27. Ingersoll, *The Works of Robert G. Ingersoll*, 379.
28. "George Jacob Holyoake," *Blue Grass Blade*, 17 January 1909.
29. Russell, *Why I Am Not a Christian*, 22.
30. Rage Against The Machine, "Vietnow."

Russell articulated a brighter vision. For him, it was a vision with no need of God, but even that was not as essential as the absence of that crippling fear that holds people back from reaching their full potential. He claimed:

> We ought to stand up and look the world frankly in the face. We ought to make the best we can of the world, and if it is not so good as we wish, after all it will still be better than what these others have made of it in all these ages. A good world needs knowledge, kindliness, and courage; it does not need a regretful hankering after the past or a fettering of the free intelligence by the words uttered long ago by ignorant men. In needs a fearless outlook and a free intelligence. It needs hope for the future.[31]

For Russell, a "fearless outlook" was necessarily in order for us to make the right decisions and set a path for a brighter future. The tactics of the Hell Houses and end-times pop genre would have horrified him. A worldview should attract adherents with its beauty, with its logic, and with its hope. Playing to the fear of torment and punishment, in this life and the next, especially when aimed at children is ignoble and cruel.

The Bible, of course, is open to interpretation and the calls to fear God are numerous. Does this equate to an endorsement of using fear as a conversion tool? The Bible also contains verses that appear to say the very opposite. The New Testament in particular emphasizes the sacrifice of Christ born out of love for humanity. The early evangelists were motivated to spread the good news about the love of God. 1 John 4:18 states that, "There is no fear in love; but perfect love casteth out fear." Romans 8:15 holds that, "For ye have not received the spirit of bondage again to fear; but ye have received the Spirit of adoption." In 2 Timothy 1:7 it says that, "For God hath not given us the spirit of fear; but of power, and of love, and of a sound mind." There is a growing movement of progressive Christianity that does not call upon fear to win adherents and is not itself fearful of challenging traditions and re-examining long held views.

Delwin Brown, an emeritus professor of theology at the Pacific School of Religion, is quick to differentiate between progressive and liberal Christianity. While progressive Christianity defines itself in opposition to the Religious Right it should not be thought of as "liberal Christianity in disguise."[32] Brown writes that:

---

31. Russell, *Why I Am Not a Christian*, 23.
32. Brown, *What Does a Progressive Christian Believe*, 3.

> A progressive Christian perspective . . . does not minimize the Christian mandate to make the gospel relevant in each new age, and it does not object to the sciences, democracy, empirical evidence, and certainly not to reasoned inquiry. In those respects, progressive Christianity unabashedly continues the liberal Christian outlook. However, the liberals went wrong, from a progressive perspective, when reasoning based on (supposedly common) human experience became for them more than valued *tools and tests* to be utilized in shaping the inherited Christian materials; gradually it became also the *source* of liberal theology.[33]

The progressive Christian walks a narrow road indeed. She or he must make sense of modernity without the reactionary hostility of the Religious Right while avoiding the "liberal failure to keep the distinctive resources of the Christian inheritance at the centre of their reflection."[34] While Brown's distinction between progressive and liberal Christians is important, the two have considerable overlap and together present a general response from the Religious Left to the hegemonic narrative of conservative Christianity.

The rise of the Christian Left has seen a diversification of the Christian voice. Responding to the American Culture Wars, Jerry Falwell met with other conservative leaders to form a lobby group known as the Moral Majority. By 1980 the group had four million registered voters and large financial backing. This level of organization allowed the Religious Right to dominate the Christian voice for three decades. The pet issues of the Religious Right, vehement opposition to abortion and same-sex marriage, have been presented as the default Christian position, the only one that is biblically sound. New research by the Public Religion Research Institute in partnership with the Brookings Institution suggests that the tide may be changing and the Christian Left, somewhat dormant since its prominence in the civil rights movement, may achieve numerical superiority. The 2013 survey found that in the 66–88 year-old category, 47 percent identified as religious conservative, 31 percent religious moderate, 12 percent religious progressive, and 10 percent non-religious. In the 18–33 year-old category, however, the number of conservatives dropped by nearly one-third to just 17 percent. Progressives, by contrast, nearly doubled to 23 percent.[35]

---

33. Ibid., 4–5.
34. Ibid., 5.
35. Jonathan Merritt, "The Rise of the Christian Left in America," *The Atlantic*, 25 July 2013.

Atheism for Christians

The Christian Left is not as uniform or organized as the Right. Given its diverse nature and its varied support base, split between liberals and progressives, it is unlikely to present a formal united front. Regardless, with millennial Christians increasingly dissatisfied with the staunch conservatism of their parents and suspicious of ironclad support for the Republican Party in the US or the conservative Coalition in Australia, the seeds of change may already be sprouting. In an incendiary papal exhortation in 2013, Pope Francis, seen as a hero of the Christian Left, especially in comparison to his ultra-conservative predecessor, Benedict XVI, described excessive capitalism as "a new tyranny."[36] In May 2012, Barack Obama announced his support for gay marriage despite facing what was tipped to be a close election at the end of the year.[37] Obama still received strong support from Christian voters and was comfortably re-elected. In June 2014, he announced changes that would see same-sex couples who work in most federal agencies receive the same benefits as heterosexual couples.[38] The Christian Left is a driving force behind LGBTIQ rights as well as healthcare reform, climate change action, women's reproductive rights, and other issues considered anathema to the Religious Right. The Christian Left Facebook page has over 175,000 members and is a constant smorgasbord of progressive activity spearheaded by, often young, Christians.

The Greek philosopher and opponent of religion, Epicurus, is reported to have said, "It is better for you to be free of fear lying upon a pallet, than to have a golden couch and a rich table and be full of trouble."[39] The promotion of fear as a means of conversion and control is a desperate and defensive tactic that ultimately surrenders before logic. Living, as we do, on this side of Darwin, how can society go back to believing in a literal six-day creation and a young earth? Living on this side of the Women's Movement how can we go back to believing women are to be silent in church and ruled over by their husbands at home? Living on this side of the Gay Rights Movement, how can we go back to seeing our homosexual brothers and sisters as perverts or mentally ill? Like Winston Smith in George Orwell's dystopian *1984*, we might say 2+2=5 under fear of pain, but could even your

36. John Cassidy, "Pope Francis's Challenge to Global Capitalism," *New Yorker*, 3 December 2013.

37. Jackie Calmes and Peter Baker, "Obama Says Same-Sex Marriage Should Be Legal," *New York Times*, 9 May 2012.

38. Michael D. Shear, "Obama Extends Marriage Benefits to Gay Couples," *New York Times*, 30 June 2014.

39. Irvine, *On Desire*, 250.

own personal Room 101 filled with your worst fears make you truly believe it? The thought of being left behind is genuinely terrifying, especially for people with a Christian upbringing, but it is not going to make thinking people return to old prejudices or recant the scientific breakthroughs of the last century and a half. A program of fear may slow the tide of progress, but it cannot turn it. Unless Christianity openly engages in the marketplace of ideas, the old guard of the Religious Right will find themselves presiding over a fragile and ever-shrinking empire of dust and grand memories.

The politics of fear may frighten some people into certain behavioral and thought patterns, but it is not a model that can fulfill Christ's calling to have life and have it more abundantly (John 10:10). Abundant life is the anthem of the Christian Left and, as Elizabeth Stoker Bruenig has argued, it may breathe new life into social Christianity. She writes that the generational changing of the guard may signal a return to "the finest features of the Christian tradition: to resist categorization, pull hard for the oppressed and downtrodden and insist upon hope while coping with the realities of power."[40] The new Christian Left symbolize Christianity without fear. It believes in a Christianity that is not afraid of gay couples but welcomes them into the church and even behind the pulpit. It believes in a Christianity unafraid of science and new knowledge about our world and ourselves. It believes in a Christianity unafraid to challenge long-held interpretations of the Bible and acknowledge human error when it is apparent. It is a Christianity that is unafraid of sharing public space with people from other religions or no religion. It fights to protect rather than suppress the equal rights of minorities. Above all, it is a Christianity unafraid to say to the men, women, and children who have been ostracized, humiliated, ignored, discriminated against, physically and sexually abused or in any other way wronged by our faith; we are truly sorry, please forgive us.

---

40. Elizabeth Stoker Bruenig, "Rise of the Christian left: Why the Religious Right's Moment May be Ending," *Salon*, 21 July 2014.

11

Conclusion

> Doth not wisdom cry? and understanding put forth her voice? She standeth in the top of high places, by the way in the places of the paths. She crieth at the gates, at the entry of the city, at the coming in at the doors. Unto you, O men, I call; and my voice is to the sons of man. O ye simple, understand wisdom: and, ye fools, be ye of an understanding heart. Hear; for I will speak of excellent things; and the opening of my lips shall be right things. For my mouth shall speak truth; and wickedness is an abomination to my lips. All the words of my mouth are in righteousness; there is nothing froward or perverse in them. They are all plain to him that understandeth, and right to them that find knowledge.
>
> Receive my instruction, and not silver; and knowledge rather than choice gold. For wisdom is better than rubies; and all the things that may be desired are not to be compared to it. (Prov 8:1–11).

New York's Metropolitan Museum of Art, known fondly around the world as "the Met", is home to Jacques-Louis David's neoclassical masterpiece, *The Death of Socrates*. Created in 1787, the influential French painter typified the Enlightenment zeitgeist by emphasizing the value of reason and logic over emotion or tradition. Socrates is depicted calm and upright as he prepares to drink hemlock, contrasting sharply with his grief-stricken

Conclusion

followers. The young man who hands Socrates the poisoned chalice is hiding his face in despair. The old sage sits stoically. With one hand open to accept his fate, the other is raised with a pointed finger. Even as he prepares to die, he is still teaching his disciples and offering freely what knowledge he has gained. His final moments convey his life's passion; to pursue and share wisdom.

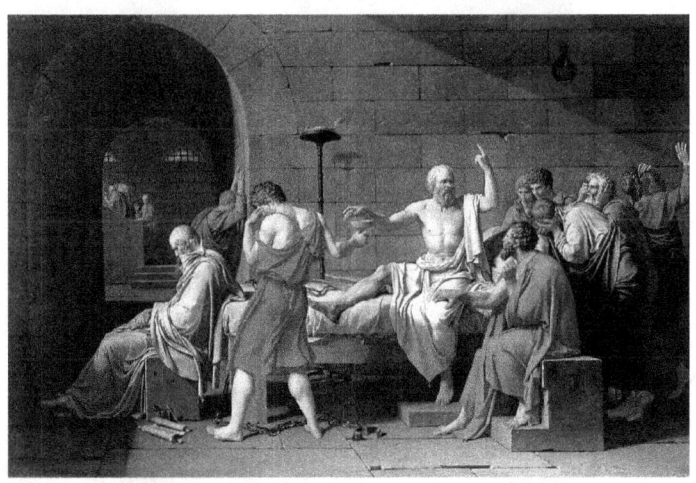

The Death of Socrates (1787) - Jacques-Louis David.

The importance of wisdom is a repeated theme throughout the Bible. It is one thing to gain knowledge, but to seek true wisdom is one of the most laudable goals in virtually every culture. The word philosophy means the love of wisdom, coming from the Greek, *philo*: to love and *sophia*: wisdom. The golden age of ancient Athens is commonly associated in Western popular consciousness with the birth of this noble pursuit, with Alfred North Whitehead famously quipping that all philosophy since is merely "a series of footnotes to Plato."[1] While Plato may well have "invented the subject of philosophy as we know it," as long as there have been homo sapiens, there have been those committed to the study of ethics, logic, nature, metaphysics, and epistemology.[2] In 1953, the prominent Austrian-British philosopher Ludwig Wittgenstein argued that "philosophy is a battle against the bewitchment of our intelligence by means of language."[3] Philosophy

1. Williams, *The Sense of the Past*, 148.
2. Ibid.
3. Thornton, *Wittgenstein on Language and Thought*, 102.

employs the medium of language to try and unpack the conceptual problems surrounding what it means to be human.

The Descent from the Cross (1614) - Peter Paul Rubens.

Plato famously charged that only a society that allowed philosophy to rule could hope for truly ethical and happy government. In *The Republic*, Socrates argues that:

> Until philosophers rule as kings in their cities, or those who are nowadays called kings and leading men become genuine and adequate philosophers so that political power and philosophy become thoroughly blended together, while the numerous natures that now pursue either one exclusively are compelled not to do so, cities will have no rest from evils.[4]

Few world leaders have ever been a paragon of the philosopher king, but it has endured as a noble ideal. At some level, we all need and use philosophy and we all have certain creeds and ethical standards that guide our behavior. To embrace philosophy, however, is to go a step further and

4. Plato, *The Republic*, 166.

Conclusion

actively explore and deconstruct the values and principles we may take for granted. Whether we wish to govern a nation or simply appraise the tenets that govern our lives, the critical eye must first be turned inward before it can hope to be of use looking outward. The ancient Delphic maxim carved on the Temple of Apollo has transcended time and place. The greatest philosophical task truly is to "know thyself." Although a firm Christian, the English poet, Alexander Pope, saw fit to write, "Know then thyself, presume not God to scan, The proper study of mankind is Man."[5]

The similarities between the death of Socrates and the death of Jesus have been highlighted since at least the second century. Emily Wilson notes that for Shelley, Socrates was "the Jesus Christ of Greece" while Voltaire regarded Jesus as "the Socrates of Palestine."[6] Both men were great teachers who wrote no books but had their words recorded by their disciples. Both were unjustly charged but refused the help of their followers to flee. Both went willingly to their deaths and forgave their killers. Plato's moving account of Socrates's last days, *Phaedo*, serves as a powerful warning against ignorance and lynch mob mentality. Despite its reputation in posterity as the cradle of Western thought, ancient Athens was a hostile place that openly persecuted many of its philosophers.[7] With religion at the heart of civic life, philosophers were routinely accused of corrupting the youth and spreading atheism. These were the charges laid against Socrates. He defended himself ably with the tools he had spent a lifetime acquiring, logic and reason, yet when the guilty verdict was passed he never entertained his followers' pleas that he escape. He surrendered himself to the city he loved and drank the hemlock.

Some 500 years later, the tragic death of Socrates deeply moved Justin Martyr, a Greek convert to Christianity. Justin used Socrates' similarities with Jesus to great affect among Greek pagans. Wilson writes:

> Socrates had already taught his disciples to reject Greek mythology and pagan religion, and exhorted people to get to know the unknown god through reason. Jesus, then, was exactly the same kind of teacher as Socrates; but he was more successful in getting his message across. Justin did not want his readers to abandon the

---

5. Pope, *The Poems of Alexander Pope*, 516.

6. Wilson, *The Death of Socrates*, 141.

7. Peter Ahrensdorf has written on the persecution of philosophers in ancient Athens and throughout Greece. See Ahrensdorf, *The Death of Socrates and the Life of Philosophy*, 9–11.

good lessons of Platonism, but to incorporate them into the new Gospel.[8]

Tertullian, born fifty-five years after Justin, fiercely condemned linking Socrates and Jesus. While Justin still saw value in the wisdom of Socrates and the Platonic tradition, for Tertullian, Socrates and philosophy more generally was corrupting and incompatible with the Christian message. For all the centuries that have passed since then, Christians still find themselves with the same choice. They can roundly reject philosophy and the wisdom of other religious and non-religious traditions and, like Tertullian, see nothing but harm and false idols everywhere except in the narrow confines of accepted dogma. Or, like Justin, they can approach ideas, new and old, with an open heart and open eyes to see the good that has come from the grand pantheon of thinking people throughout the ages.

The purpose of this book has not been simply to advocate a progressive form of Christianity, but rather to celebrate and learn from some of the greatest minds who did not subscribe to a religious faith. If there is one central theme to this work it is that Christians must resist the temptation to deify tradition and to worship the cultural form and function that makes them comfortable. Christians, to be truly worthy of name, must follow the example of their eponymous founder and be tenaciously committed to the truth, even if this means challenging the established orthodoxy. Truth itself is at the heart of Christianity. In Jesus' dramatic confrontation with Pilate, he says, "for this cause came I into the world, that I should bear witness unto the truth" (John 8:37). But we must reply in turn, as Pilate did; "what is truth?" Trapped within our mortal coil, with finite brains and limited consciousness, perhaps some of the great universal truths are simply beyond our comprehension. What seems clear, however, is that Christians cannot simply open the Bible and find readymade answers to all the intricate problems of everyday life. Further, it is not enough to defer to certain literalist interpretations of the Bible when they stand obnoxious to reason. One of the best known biblical aphorisms holds that "the truth shall set you free" (John 8:32). This is a beautiful sentiment, but must not be interpreted as meaning that Christians are free from critical thinking if they hold to simple truths.

When exploring some of the important public issues that face society, it is not adequate to fall back on tradition as a substitute for critical thought and a *de facto* argument. Tevye the Milkman opens *Fiddler on the Roof* with

---

8. Wilson, *The Death of Socrates*, 145–46.

the following statement, "And how do we keep our balance? That I can tell you in one word: tradition!" While the quote refers specifically to Judaism, it is equally applicable to Christianity. Tradition acts as a vital part of the grid that provides us with a sense of self and community. Religions use tradition to identify and differentiate themselves, just as nations do and even individual families. Traditions spring up in most areas of life and they often enjoy an unnaturally lengthy lifespan. Long after its usefulness has expired a tradition may be continued for the very fact that it is a tradition.

The United States still holds its presidential elections on a Tuesday. When this practice began it was designed to be convenient for the large agricultural population who were often required to work and trade on weekends. Today the rule actually makes voting inconvenient for the bulk of the population. Why then is it maintained? Why do special so-called royal families still live in palaces with enormous public contributions in democratic countries? Why do people kiss under mistletoe? Why do footballers swap shirts at the end of big matches? Why do we associate blue with boys and pink with girls? Why do doctoral graduates still don medieval garb? Tradition has a strange and ominous power. It can delight and blind in equal measures. Needless to say, some traditions are powerful and instructive. Others are charming and endearing, even if they serve little purpose. Others still are potentially dangerous and harmful. In particular, the traditional gender binary is subtly entwined in many cultural traditions observed in the Western world. In a modernity that holds sacred the essential equality of all people regardless of gender, race, or sexual orientation, some Christian traditions send a very twisted message.

Friedrich Nietzsche argued that tradition can be a form of bondage where the customs and ideas of great leaders from the past are valued at the expense of progress and innovation. Those who hold fanatically to tradition, he suggests, are crippled by an irrational fear of change. They do not simply seek to honor the past but to thwart the possibly of a better future. In his 1876 work, *On the Uses and Disadvantage of History for Life*, he argues:

> Monumental history is the masquerade in which their hatred for the powerful and great of their own age is disguised as bloated admiration for the powerful and great of past ages. Thereby they invert the real meaning of this historical viewpoint into its opposite. Whether they are aware of it or not, they act as though their motto were: let the dead bury the living.[9]

9. Fritzsche, *Nietzsche and the Death of God*, 61.

Atheism for Christians

Uncertainty is the necessary fellow traveller or great change. Nietzsche argued that, "All great things, in order to inscribe eternal demands in the heart of humanity, must first wander the earth under monstrous and terrifying masks."[10] It takes courage and conviction to challenge long-standing traditions and new ideas may indeed seem frightening, but such is the price of meaningful change.

The Christian church has many beautiful and worthwhile traditions that serve as powerful reminders of the core message; love, forgiveness, and redemption. Every aspect of the traditional Mass is imbued with meaning, just as the rituals of the newer denominations are all significant. Jesus said that, "The thief cometh not, but for to steal, and to kill, and to destroy: I am come that they might have life, and that they might have it more abundantly" (John 10:10). This should provide a crucial litmus test for Christians. Which customs and traditions enhance life, inspire kindness, and encourage love and inclusion? Do some promote fear, tribalism, and exclusion? The late iconoclast Christopher Hitchens famously charged that "religion poisons everything" in his influential bestseller, *God is not Great*.[11] Rather than defensively ignoring a perceived attack, Christians should examine the criticisms and explore the evidence presented. Only the proud refuse to entertain the notion that they could be wrong, or need to improve in some areas.

We live in a completely different world to the one of Jesus and the Bible writers. Through ground-breaking scientific discoveries, we understand the mechanics of volcanoes, earthquakes, floods, and other acts of nature that would have seemed divinely caused to the Bible heroes. We know also how fragile our planet is and understand, if it is destroyed, it will not likely be an act of celestial fury, but the sorry result of our own mismanagement. Although it is not always the reality, we live in a world that at least holds the standard that men and women are equal and that slavery is wrong. Both concepts were unthinkable 2000 years ago. The Bible is the sacred text of Christianity, but it must not be deified or given authority it does not give itself. It must not be divorced from the historical circumstances and context of its creation. It cannot be seen as a simple rule book; impervious to criticism or common sense. In *Rescuing the Bible from Fundamentalism*, Bishop Spong writes that:

10. Nietzsche, *Beyond Good and Evil*, 3.
11. Hitchens, *God is not Great*.

> Those whose religious security is rooted in a literal Bible do not want that security disturbed. They are not happy when facts challenge their biblical understanding or when nuances in the text are introduced or when they are forced to deal with either contradictions or changing insights. The Bible, as they understand it, shares in the permanence and certainty of God, convinces them that they right, and justifies the enormous fear and even negativity that lie so close to the surface in the fundamentalistic religion. For biblical literalists, there is always an enemy to be defeated in mortal combat.[12]

Bibleanity negates the love that sits above even faith and hope as the greatest Christian virtue (1 Cor 13:13). It causes otherwise rational, sensitive people to become defensive to the point of paranoia. All who do not submit to their precise interpretation of ancient texts, translated many times over, in regard to modern situations inconceivable to the original authors, are seen as lost souls at best, if not tools of the devil.

Some Christian apologists, especially literalists, fall back on the famous Pascalian wager. Although only a paragraph in the larger work *Pensées* (Thoughts) by the seventeenth-century French philosopher and mathematician, Blaise Pascal, the wager has been a staple of the apologist community for centuries. Pascal insists that the question of God's existence is beyond science and reason. He writes:

> Let us then examine this point, and say, "God is, or He is not." But to which side shall we incline? Reason can decide nothing here. ... Let us weigh the gain and loss in wagering that God is. Let us estimate these two chances. If you gain, you gain all; if you lose, you lose nothing. Wager, then, without hesitation that He is.[13]

The wager is often misunderstood by Fundamentalists, who reduce it to little more than a silly bet by essentially saying, believe us, just in case. This simplistic approach invites ridicule. By the same logic, you may as well join the Pastafarians and worship the Flying Spaghetti Monster, just in case.[14]

Pascal is not saying we must slavishly follow an ultra-conservative, anti-science, anti-women, anti-tolerance version of Christianity because if we are right, God will reward our mindless devotion and if we are wrong, it will not matter as we are dead. Pascal's argument is that a Christian who

---

12. Spong, *Rescuing the Bible from Fundamentalism*, 2.
13. Pascal, *Pensées*, 66–67.
14. Henderson, *The Gospel of the Flying Spaghetti Monster*.

follows the highest principles of the faith, to live a life marked by radical and unselfish love of others, can never be the loser. By doing so, even if God does not exist, we would have lived a life exhibiting the fruits of the Spirit; love, joy, peace, longsuffering, gentleness, goodness, faith, meekness and temperance (Gal 5:22–23). But the onus is on Christians to ensure the faith they represent is one that uplifts and encourages, that enhances life.

The Christian church has so much beauty in its philosophical and theological traditions and these in turn have inspired some of the greatest works of beauty in architecture, painting, sculpture, and music. Hans Urs Von Balthasar, the influential Swiss theologian and Catholic priest, insisted that love and beauty were central to Christian transcendence. His well-known quote on the experience of beauty holds that:

> Before the beautiful—no, not really *before* but *within* the beautiful—the whole person quivers. He not only "finds" the beautiful moving; rather, he experiences himself as being moved and possessed by it.[15]

Christianity is beautiful, yet, like Dr. Jekyll and Mr. Hyde, there is a dark side too. There is the side that exploits the poor and abuses the innocent. There is the side that craves money and power. There is the side that draws its strength from the politics of fear. Christianity at its worst is truly as ugly as the sins it condemns. It lashes outward like a spoiled child, refuses to see its own faults, and damns for eternity those who do not fit into its rigid mold of righteousness, cast in its own petty image. It drives young gay teens to suicide by telling them that their very nature, their essential self, is an abomination to God. It tells women they exist to submit to their husbands and produce children, and measures their worth by maternal obedience. It tells its brightest minds to immediately dismiss all science and academic knowledge that may challenge any comfortable orthodoxies. Christianity is the world's largest religion, with one in three people on the planet identifying with it. This perverted form of Christianity, which substitutes forgiveness with condemnation, acceptance with exclusivity, and love with intolerance, should not be allowed to dominate the discourse. There is too much at stake. We must fight for a God of love.

Atheism too, like Oscar Wilde's *Portrait of Dorian Gray*, has both a beautiful and a horrible face. Atheism at its worst is a militant ideology which heeds the call of American Atheists president, David Silverman, and

---

15. Schindler, *Hans Urs Von Balthasar*, 124.

shows "zero tolerance" to competing views.[16] Like Richard Dawkins, the brilliant scientist whose unfettered loathing of religion has caused him to become more a hollow caricature of rage than a respected public intellectual; the motto of militant atheism is "ridicule and show contempt" to your opponents.[17] Atheism does have zealous evangelists and fundamentalist culture warriors who do not seek honest discourse but obedient discipleship. At the epicentre of atheistic meanness, all dissenters are to be belittled and humiliated. Like its Christian counterpart, it thrives in a culture of fear. Atheism at its best, however, could not be more different. It is a worldview that champions critical thinking, academic debate, open discussion, and reason. It looks at the problems facing the world and seeks practical solutions. Having no recourse to the supernatural, it draws on our common humanity as the binding force that should bring all people together to champion the common good and to leave our children a better world than the one we inherited. It is a philosophy that boasts some of the greatest minds to ever live. As this book has argued, it would be utterly foolish to ignore their wisdom.

Both Christianity and atheism have intellectual giants in their ranks. Both worldviews can draw on the politics of fear and exclusion and both, at their best, can seek a better existence through open dialogue, mutual respect, and cooperation. There is an old Native American story said to be of Cherokee origin called Two Wolves.[18] The setting is a respected elder teaching his young grandson an important life lesson. The story goes:

> The grandfather explains to the young boy that we all have a battle going on inside of us. He said, "My son, the battle is between two wolves that live inside us all. One is evil. It is anger, envy, jealousy, sorrow, regret, greed, arrogance, self-pity, guilt, resentment, inferiority, lies, false pride, superiority and ego. The other is good. It is joy, peace, love, hope, serenity, humility, kindness, benevolence, empathy, generosity, truth, compassion and faith."

---

16. Cathy Lynn Grossman. "Richard Dawkins to Atheist Rally: 'Show Contempt' for Faith," *USA Today*, 25 March 2012.

17. Ibid. Dawkins was speaking at a Reason Rally at the Washington Monument and was specifically referring to Catholics who believe in transubstantiation when he called for ridicule and contempt to be shown by atheists.

18. Douglas Fry has noted that there is no compelling evidence to confirm the origins of the story, but its value as a generic folk tale remains. Fry, *War, Peace, and Human Nature*, 37.

Atheism for Christians

> The grandson thought about it for a minute and then asked his grandfather: "Which wolf wins?" The old Cherokee replied simply, "The one you feed."[19]

We cannot choose which wolf people with another worldview will feed. We cannot even control which wolf people who share our worldview will feed. We can only control ourselves. What kind of Christianity will I represent?

Catholic psychologist Peter C. Morea also identifies two distinct brands of Christianity, Catholicism in particular, and suggests there is an intellectual contest at work for supremacy. In *Towards a Liberal Catholicism*, he uses depth psychology to distinguish the liberal and authoritarian wings of the church.[20] Morea argues that an outward display of absolute certainty and a staunch intolerance to hearing other views is often a manifestation of unconscious doubt. If we allow ourselves to contemplate the possibility of being wrong in some areas and remain open to intelligent discourse; we become free to discuss important issues and learn from great minds. If not, we risk becoming exclusive, hostile, and aggressive, needing to constantly be around those who share and reaffirm our ideas. The American existential philosopher Rollo May held that:

> People who claim to be absolutely convinced that their stand is the only right one are dangerous. Such conviction is the essence not only of dogmatism, but of its more destructive cousin, fanaticism. It blocks off the user from learning new truth, and it is a dead giveaway of unconscious doubt. The person then has to double his or her protests in order to quiet not only the opposition but his or her own unconscious doubts as well.[21]

In Harper Lee's classic novel, *To Kill a Mockingbird*, Miss Maudie critiques Christian fundamentalism, claiming, "sometimes the Bible in the hand of one man is worse than a whiskey bottle."[22] She continues, "there are just some kind of men . . . who're so busy worrying about the next world they've never learned to live in this one, and you can look down the street and see the results."[23] Like the classic Bob Dylan folk song, *With God on Our Side*, Lee is highlighting the great potential for tragedy when Christianity

19. Andrea Wachter, "Which Wolf Are You Feeding?," *Huffington Post*, 22 November 2013.
20. Morea, *Towards a Liberal Catholicism*.
21. May, *The Courage to Create*, 9.
22. Bloom, *Harper Lee's To Kill a Mockingbird*, 181.
23. Ibid.

Conclusion

(or one version thereof) is believed without question and enforced without challenge.

Bertrand Russell's famous 1948 debate on the existence of God with the Jesuit priest Frederick C. Copleston helped popularize the agnostic position in a highly Christian society. For Russell, doubt was not a weakness but a safeguard against extremism. In his *Unpopular Essays*, he posits that:

> Most of the greatest evils that man has inflicted upon man have come through people feeling quite certain about something which, in fact, was false. To know the truth is more difficult than most men suppose, and to act with ruthless determination in the belief that truth is the monopoly of their party is to invite disaster.[24]

One of the greatest statements of faith in the Bible comes from the father of the possessed boy. The story recounts that, "Jesus said unto him, If thou canst believe, all things are possible to him that believeth. And straightway the father of the child cried out, and said with tears, Lord, I believe; help thou mine unbelief" (Mark 9:23–24). Acknowledging doubt is not a negation of faith or a surrender of values. It is an honest acceptance of the human condition.

Christians, and indeed all people, should regularly examine their worldview and be prepared to challenge aspects that cannot be reasonably justified. The way in which Christianity is practiced today is profoundly different to the early church in many respects. As society has evolved and changed so too has the church, and even today there is enormous variety in form, function, rite, and ritual. Christians will never agree on all aspects of theology, but it is vital that ideas can at least be discussed and challenged so that, as a faith community, the church can continue to grow and prosper. Gene Robinson has said that, "God calls all of his children to the table. We can disagree and even say a lot of hateful things, but what we can't do in good conscience is leave the table. Or demand that someone else not be at the table."[25] However convinced we may be of our position, there is an inherent value in hearing other voices and being brave enough to question why.

This book has presented a number of intellectual giants from the secular tradition in order to highlight some key areas where atheism can be rightly proud of its contribution to humanity. Christians should not be

---

24. Russell, *Unpopular Essays*, 176.
25. "Gene Robinson: It Is a Sin to Treat Me This Way," *Telegraph*, 29 April 2008.

afraid to learn from the secular tradition but should be quick to appreciate great minds, whatever their religious position. Whether new ideas are accepted, rejected, or modified, we must always be willing to scrutinize that which is held sacred to ensure it deserves a position of reverence. Although the Western world, with the possible exception of the United States, is often seen as post-Christian, there is still so much this rich religious tradition can offer. Similarly, the Christian world can and should learn from the best atheist thinkers. The great truths of the Christian faith are eternal, but society is not static and many aspects of the church must be willing to change in order to retain relevance in a dynamic, interconnected world. Christianity can be a global force for good, but it must be inclusive and loving. Christian leaders should be at the vanguard of the fight against racism, misogyny, and homophobia. It is a tragedy that so often the church is seen as enabler of prejudice and bigotry. With courage and compassion, Christianity must defend the nexus of faith and reason and be willing to abandon even long held traditions that do not hold up to scrutiny. The great works from the secular pantheon should be known by all thinking Christians. As ever, we should take the advice of Romans 12:9 and "abhor what is evil", but we should also "cleave to what is good." It should not matter where we find that goodness.

Bibliography

ABC News, "1 in 8 Australians Living in Poverty: Report." Online: http://www.abc.net.au/news/2012-10-14/1-in-8-australians-living-in-poverty/4312154.
———. "Anglican Church Denies New Wedding Vows are Sexist." Online: http://www.abc.net.au/news/2012-08-25/anglican-church-denies-new-wedding-vows-are-sexist/4222654.
———. "Budget 2014: Funding for Secular Counsellors Cut in School Chaplaincy Program." Online: http://www.abc.net.au/news/2014-05-15/cut-to-secular-advisors-program-in-federal-budget/5455176.
Ahrensdorf, Peter J. *The Death of Socrates and the Life of Philosophy: An Interpretation of Plato's Phaedo*. Albany, NY: State University of New York Press, 1995.
Ali, Ayaan Hirsi. *The Caged Virgin: An Emancipation Proclamation for Women and Islam*. New York: Free, 2008.
Alston, Jon P. *The Scientific Case against Scientific Creationism*. Lincoln, NE: iUniverse, 2003.
Anderson, Dean A. "The Original Left Behind." Online: http://www.christianitytoday.com/ct/2012/marchweb-only/originalleftbehind.html.
Anderson, Ralph E., et al., *Human Behavior and the Social Environment: A Social Systems Approach*. Edison, NJ: Transaction, 2009.
Appleyard, Bryan. *The Brain is Wider Than the Sky: Why Simple Solutions Don't Work in a Complex World*. London: Weidenfeld & Nicolson, 2011.
Aquinas, Thomas. *Summa Contra Gentiles*. South Bend, IN: University of Notre Dame Press, 2003.
Atheist Foundation. "Opening Video—2012 Global Atheist Convention." Online: http://www.youtube.com/watch?v=s3OtBFisK-g.
Australia Institute. "Youth Survey 2013 Election—Issues & Policies." Online: http://www.tai.org.au/content/youth-survey-2013-election-issues-policies.
Australian Bureau of Statistics. "Reflecting a Nation: Stories from the 2011 Census." Online: http://www.abs.gov.au/ausstats/abs@.nsf/Latestproducts/2071.0Main%20Features902012%E2%80%932013.
Bagemihl, Bruce. *Biological Exuberance: Animal Homosexuality and Natural Diversity*. New York: St. Martin's, 2010.
Balibar, Etienne. *The Philosophy of Marx*. London: Verso, 1995.

Bibliography

Banner, Michael. *Christian Ethics and Contemporary Moral Problems*. Cambridge: Cambridge University Press, 2003.
Barker, Dan. *Godless: How an Evangelical Preacher Became One of America's Leading Atheists*. Berkeley, CA: Ulysses, 2008.
———. *The Good Atheist: Living a Purpose-Filled Life Without God*. Berkeley, CA: Ulysses, 2011.
Barna Group. "Abortion Continues to Split the Nation." Online: http://www.barna.org/culture-articles/394-new-barna-study-explores-current-views-on-abortion-.
———. "New Marriage and Divorce Statistics Released." Online: http://www.barna.org/barna-update/article/15-familykids/42-new-marriage-and-divorce-statistics-released#.Uxkn7D-SwfU.
Beliefnet. "Worse Than Hell: Christopher Hitchens on the Religious Mind." Online: http://www.beliefnet.com/Entertainment/Books/2007/05/Worse-Than-Hell-Christopher-Hitchens-On-The-Religious-Mind.aspx#cTJ4DFlo4xhYB838.99.
Bentham, Jeremy. *Introduction to Principles of Morals and Legislation*. Oxford: Clarendon, 1079.
Benson, Rod. "Five Reasons to Oppose Same-Sex Marriage." Online: http://rodbenson.com/2012/08/25/five-reasons-to-oppose-same-sex-marriage/
Bivins, Jason C. *Religion of Fear: The Politics of Horror in Conservative Evangelicalism*. Oxford: Oxford University Press, 2008.
Blackburn, Simon. *Think: A Compelling Introduction to Philosophy*. Oxford: Oxford University Press, 1999.
Bloom, Harold. *Harper Lee's To Kill a Mockingbird*. New York: Chelsea House, 2007.
Blumenthal, Max. *Republican Gomorrah: Inside the Movement that Shattered the Party*. New York: Nation, 2009.
Boer, Roland. *Criticism of Religion: On Marxism and Theology*. Leiden: Koninklijke Brill, 2009.
Bonnefoy, Yves. *Asian Mythologies*. Chicago: University of Chicago Press, 1993.
Booth, Robert. "Richer Than St. Paul's: Church That Attracts 8,000 Congregation to a Disused Cinema," *The Guardian*, 11 April 2009
Bovell, Carlos R. *Rehabilitating Inerrancy in a Culture of Fear*. Eugene, OR: Wipf and Stock, 2012.
Brewster, Melanie. "Atheism, Gender and Sexuality." In *The Oxford Handbook of Atheism*, edited by Stephen Bullivant and Michael Ruse, 511–24. Oxford: Oxford University Press, 2013.
Brown, Callum G. *The Death of Christian Britain: Understanding Secularisation 1800–2000*. London: Routledge, 2001.
Brown, Callum G., and Michael Snape. *Secularisation in the Christian World*. Farnham, UK: Ashgate, 2010.
Brown, Delwin. *What Does a Progressive Christian Believe?: A Guide for the Searching, the Open, and the Curious*. New York: Church, 2008.
Buck-Morss, Susan. *Hegel, Haiti, and Universal History*. Pittsburgh: University of Pittsburgh Press, 2009.
Canseco, Mario. *Creationism and Evolution*. New York: Angus Reid Public Opinion, 2012.
Carey, George. "Tolerating Religion." In *The Politics of Toleration: Tolerance and Intolerance in Modern Life*, edited by Susan Mendus, 45–64. Edinburgh: Edinburgh University Press, 1999.

Bibliography

Carpenter, Dale. *Flagrant Conduct: The Story of Lawrence v. Texas.* New York: Norton, 2012.

Carson, Ben. *Gifted Hands: The Ben Carson Story.* Grand Rapids: Zondervan, 1990.

Causevic, Fikret. *The Global Crisis of 2008 and Keynes's General Theory.* New York: Springer, 2015.

CBS Denver. "Judge Orders Colorado Cake Maker to Serve Gay Couples." Online: http://denver.cbslocal.com/2013/12/06/judge-orders-colorado-cake-maker-to-serve-gay-couples/

Chappell, Louise, et al. *The Politics of Human Rights in Australia.* Melbourne: Cambridge University Press, 2009.

Christianity Today. "Hillsong New York Pastor Carl Lentz: We Have a Lot of Gay Men and Women in Our Church and I Pray We Always Do." Online: http://www.christiantoday.com/article/hillsong.new.york.pastor.carl.lentz.we.have.a.lot.of.gay.men.and.women.in.our.church.and.i.pray.we.always.do/37918.htm.

―――. "Is Christianity Good for the World." Online: http://www.christianitytoday.com/ct/2007/mayweb-only/119-42.0.html.

Chryssides, George D. *Historical Dictionary of New Religious Movements.* Plymouth, UK: Scarecrow, 2012.

Clauss-Ehlers, Caroline S., et al., eds. *Handbook of Culturally Responsive School Mental Health.* New York: Springer, 2013.

CNN. "Ten Commandments Monument Moved." Online: http://edition.cnn.com/2003/LAW/08/27/ten.commandments/.

Collins, Francis. *The Language of God: A Scientist Presents Evidence for Belief.* New York: Free, 2007.

Continetti, Matthew. *The Persecution of Sarah Palin: How the Elite Media Tried to Bring Down a Rising Star.* New York: Sentinel, 2009.

Conway, John S. *The Nazi Persecution of the Churches, 1933–1945.* Toronto: Ryerson, 1968.

Cooper, Terry. *Handbook of Administrative Ethics.* New York: Marcel Dekker, 2001.

Cornwall, Susannah. *Theology and Sexuality.* London: SCM, 2013.

Council for American Private Education. "Facts and Studies." Online: http://www.capenet.org/facts.html.

Countryman, L. William. *Dirt, Greed, and Sex: Sexual Ethics in the New Testament and Their Implications for Today.* Minneapolis: Fortress, 2007.

Craig, William Lane. "Contemporary Moral Arguments." Online: http://www.reasonablefaith.org/contemporary-moral-arguments.

Cronk, Harold. *God's Not Dead.* Scottsdale, PA: Pure Flix, 2014.

Cuidon. Jackson. "Left Behind: Not a 'Christian Movie.' Not Even Close." Online: http://www.christianitytoday.com/ct/2014/october-web-only/left-behind.html?start=3.

Dalrymple, Brent. *The Age of the Earth.* Stanford: Stanford University Press, 1991.

Darwin, Charles. *On the Origin of Species.* London: Penguin, 2009.

Davidson, Lucy, and Markku Linnoila. *Risk Factors for Youth Suicide.* New York: Routledge, 2011.

Dawkins, Richard. *The God Delusion.* London: Bantam, 2006.

―――. "Quotes." Online: http://richarddawkins.net/quotes/47

De Beauvoir, Simone. *The Second Sex.* London: Vintage, 1997.

De Botton, Alain. *Religion for Atheists: A Non-Believer's Guide to the Uses of Religion.* New York: Random House, 2012.

Delirious? *King of Fools.* Furious? Records, 1997.

Bibliography

Dennett, Daniel. *Breaking the Spell: Religion as a Natural Phenomenon*. New York: Viking, 2006.

DeRogatis, Amy. *Saving Sex: Sexuality and Salvation in American Evangelicalism*. New York: Oxford University Press, 2015.

Deveney, Catherine, "Atheist Alphabet." Online: https://www.youtube.com/watch?v=DmIHMLN5G0A.

Discover Christian Schools. "Why Should I Consider Christian Education?" Online: http://www.discoverchristianschools.com/learn_about/10_reasons_to_send_your_child_to_a_christian_school.

Doane, Darren. *Collision: Is Christianity Good for the World?* Beverley Hills, CA: LEVEL4, 2009.

Doumit, Peter E. *A Unification of Science and Religion*. Pittsburgh: RoseDog, 2010.

Dulles, Avery. *A History of Apologetics*. San Francisco: Ignatius, 2005.

Dundes, Alan. *The Flood Myth*. Berkeley: University of California Press, 1988.

Dylan, Bob. *The Times They Are a-Changin'*. Columbia Records, 1964.

Dynes, Wayne R., and Stephen Donaldson. *Homosexuality and Government, Politics and Prisons*. New York: Taylor and Francis, 1992.

Eco, Umberto, *The Limits of Interpretation*. Bloomington, IN: Indiana University Press, 1994.

Einstein, Albert. *Albert Einstein, The Human Side: Glimpses from His Archives*. Princeton: Princeton University Press, 2013.

Emam, Moataz H. *Are We There Yet?: The Search for a Theory of Everything*. Sharjah, UAE: Bentham, 2011.

Eskridge, Larry. *God's Forever Family: The Jesus People Movement in America*. Oxford: Oxford University Press, 2013.

Estep, William R. *Renaissance and Reformation*. Grand Rapids: Eerdmans, 1986.

Feser, Edward. *The Last Superstition: A Refutation of the New Atheism*. South Bend, IN: St. Augustine's, 2008.

Freire, Paulo. *Pedagogy of the Oppressed*. New York: Continuum, 2000.

Fritzsche, Peter. *Nietzsche and the Death of God: Selected Writings*. Long Grove, IL: Waveland, 2013.

Fry, Douglas P. *War, Peace, and Human Nature: The Convergence of Evolutionary and Cultural Views*. Oxford: Oxford University Press, 2013.

Galaxy Research. "Religion and Same-Sex Marriage." Online: http://www.australianmarriageequality.com/wp/wp-content/uploads/2012/03/REPORT-Religion-And-Same-Sex-Marriage-Feb-2012.pdf.

Gallup. "In U.S., 46% Hold Creationist View of Human Origins." Online: http://www.gallup.com/poll/155003/Hold-Creationist-View-Human-Origins.aspx?version=print.

Godwin, William. *Memoirs and Posthumous Works of Mary Wollstonecraft Godwin*. Vol. 1. Dublin: Burnside, 1798.

Gopal, Sarvepalli. *Selected Works of Jawaharlal Nehru*. Series 1, Vol. 2. New Delhi: Orient Longman, 1972.

———. *Selected Works of Jawaharlal Nehru*. Series 1, Vol. 3. New Delhi: Orient Longman, 1972.

Gorman, G. E. "Series Foreword." In *Feminism and Christian Tradition: An Annotated Bibliography and Critical Introduction to the Literature*, edited by Mary-Paula Walsh, ix–x. Westport, CT: Greenwood, 1999.

Bibliography

Gowans, Chris. "Moral Relativism." Online: http://plato.stanford.edu/entries/moral-relativism/.
Gould, Stephen Jay. "Impeaching a Self-Appointed Judge." *Scientific American* 267, July 1992, 118–21.
———. *Leonardo's Mountain of Clams and the Diet of Worms: Essays on Natural History*. Cambridge: Harvard University Press, 2011.
Grady, J. Lee. *Ten Lies the Church Tells Women*. Lake Mary, FL: Charisma House, 2006.
Grenz, Stanley J. *The Moral Quest: Foundations of Christian Ethics*. Downers Grove, IL: IVP, 2000.
Gribben, Crawford. *Writing the Rapture: Prophecy Fiction in Evangelical America*. Oxford: Oxford University Press, 2009.
Gudorf, Christine E. *Body, Sex, and Pleasure: Reconstructing Christian Sexual Ethics*. Cleveland, OH: Pilgrim, 1995.
Guenther, Bruce L. "Ethnicity and Evangelical Protestants in Canada." In *Christianity and Ethnicity in Canada*, edited by Paul Bramadat and David Seljak, 365–414. Toronto: University of Toronto Press, 2008.
Gundry, Robert H. *Matthew: A Commentary on His Literary and Theological Art*. Grand Rapids, Eerdmans, 1982.
Ham, Ken. *Demolishing Supposed Bible Contradictions*. Vol. 1. Green Forrest, AR: Master, 2010.
Harvey, David. *A Companion to Marx's Capital*. Vol. 1. London: Verso, 2010.
Harris, Sam. *The End of Faith: Religion, Terror, and the Future of Reason*. New York: Norton, 2004.
Harrison, Peter. *The Bible, Protestantism, and the Rise of Natural Science*. Cambridge: Cambridge University Press, 2001.
Hegel, G. W. F. *The Philosophy of History*. Mineola, NY: Dove, 2004.
Heit, Helmut. "Nietzsche's Genealogy of Early Greek Philosophy." In *Nietzsche as a Scholar of Antiquity*, edited by Anthony K. Jensen and Helmut Heit, 217–32. London: Bloomsbury, 2014.
Henderson, Bobby. *The Gospel of the Flying Spaghetti Monster*. New York: Villard, 2006.
Hess, Beth B., et al. *Sociology*. Boston: Allyn and Bacon, 1996.
Hitchens, Christopher. *God is Not Great: How Religion Poisons Everything*. New York: Twelve, 2007.
Hitchens, Christopher, and Douglas Wilson. *Is Christianity Good for the World?* Moscow, ID: Canon, 2008.
Hobbes, Thomas. *Leviathan*. Cambridge: Cambridge University Press, 1996.
Hofstadter, Richard. *Anti-Intellectualism in American Life*. New York: Vintage, 1963.
Hume, David. *Hume: Dialogues concerning Natural Religion: And Other Writings*. Cambridge: Cambridge University Press, 2007.
Hutchinson, Mark, and John Wolffe. *A Short History of Global Evangelicalism*. Cambridge: Cambridge University Press, 2012.
Ingersoll, Robert G. *The Works of Robert G. Ingersoll*. Vol. 12. New York: Ingersoll, 1900.
Irvine, William B. *On Desire: Why We Want What We Want*. Oxford: Oxford University Press, 2006.
Jackson, Gregory S. *The Word and Its Witness: The Spiritualization of American Realism*. Chicago: University of Chicago Press, 2009.
Jensen, Michael. "Have Evangelicals Lost Their Minds?" Online: http://sydneyanglicans.net/blogs/culture/have-evangelicals-lost-their-minds.

Bibliography

John Paul II. "Mulieris Dignitatem." Online: http://www.vatican.va/holy_father/john_paul_ii/apost_letters/documents/hf_jp-ii_apl_15081988_mulieris-dignitatem_en.html.

———. "Ordinatio Sacerdotalis." Online: http://www.vatican.va/holy_father/john_paul_ii/apost_letters/1994/documents/hf_jp-ii_apl_19940522_ordinatio-sacerdotalis_en.html.

Jones, Benjamin T., *Republicanism and Responsible Government: The Shaping of Australia and Canada*. Montreal: McGill-Queen's University Press, 2014.

Jones, Jeffrey M. "In U.S., 3 in 10 Say They Take the Bible Literally." Online: http://www.gallup.com/poll/148427/say-bible-literally.aspx.

Joshi, S. T. *H. L. Mencken on Religion*. Amherst, NY: Prometheus, 2002.

Kiesewetter, Hubert. "Ethical Foundations of Popper's Philosophy." In *Karl Popper: Philosophy and Problems*, edited by Anthony O'Hear, 275–88. Cambridge: Cambridge University Press, 1995.

Kinnaman, David. *You Lost Me: Why Young Christians Are Leaving Church . . . and Rethinking Faith*. Grand Rapids: Baker, 2011.

Kipling, Rudyard. *The Collected Poems of Rudyard Kipling*. Ware, UK: Wordsworth, 1994.

Kiser, Randall. *Beyond Right and Wrong: The Power of Effective Decision Making for Attorneys and Clients*. New York: Springer, 2010.

Knowles, Elizabeth. *What They Didn't Say—A Book of Misquotations*. Oxford: Oxford University Press, 2006.

Kotva, Joseph J. *The Christian Case for Virtue Ethics*. Washington, DC: Georgetown University Press, 1996.

Kramer, Heinrich, and James Sprenger. *Malleus Maleficarum*. New York: Cosimo, 2007.

Kulke, Hermann, and Dietmar Rothermund. *A History of India*. 4th ed. London: Routledge, 2004.

Kvam, Kristen E., et al. *Eve and Adam: Jewish, Christian, and Muslim Readings on Genesis and Gender*. Bloomington, IN: Indiana University Press, 1999.

Kyle, Richard G. *Apocalyptic Fever: End-Time Prophecies in Modern America*. Eugene, OR: Cascade, 2012.

Laidler, Harry W. *History of Socialism: An Historical Comparative Study of Socialism, Communism, Utopia*. London: Routledge, 2007.

Lakewood Church. "Leadership Team." Online: http://www.lakewoodchurch.com/Pages/new-here/Leadership-Team.aspx.

Le Beau, Bryan F. *The Atheist: Madalyn Murray O'Hair*. New York: New York University Press, 2003.

Lewis, C. S. *Mere Christianity*. London: Harper-Collins, 2002.

Levack, Brian. *The Witch Hunt in Early Modern Europe*. 3rd ed. London: Longman, 2006.

Lienesch, Michael. *In the Beginning: Fundamentalism, the Scopes Trial, and the Making of the Antievolution Movement*. Chapel Hill:, NC University of North Carolina Press, 2007.

Life Way. "Top Ten Risks of Having Sex before Marriage." Online: http://www.lifeway.com/Article/sexuality-true-love-waits-tlw-Top-ten-risks-of-having-sex-before-marriage

Manning, Christel. "Atheism, Secularity, the Family and Children." In *Atheism and Secularity, Vol. 1 & 2*, edited by Phil Zuckerman, 19–42. Santa Barbara: Greenwood, 2010.

Bibliography

Marcotte, Amanda. "How the Christian Right's Homophobia Scares Away Religious Young People." Online: http://www.alternet.org/story/155462/how_the_christian_right%27s_homophobia_scares_away_religious_young_people
Marcovitz, Hal. *Suicide*. Edina, MN: ABDO, 2010.
Marsden, George M. *Understanding Fundamentalism and Evangelicalism*. Grand Rapids: Eerdmans, 1991.
Marx, Karl. *Critique of Hegel's "Philosophy Of Right."* Melbourne: Cambridge University Press, 1982.
———. *Early Writings*. London: Penguin Classics, 1992.
———. *Karl Marx: Selected Writings*. Oxford: Oxford University Press, 2000.
Marx, Karl, and Frederick Engels. *The Communist Manifesto: Manifesto of the Communist Party*. Sydney: Australian Socialist Party, 1920.
May, Rollo. *The Courage to Create*. New York: Bantam, 1980.
McCay, Brent. *Confessions of a Heretic: How a Right Wing, Fundamentalist, Conservative Pastor Became a Leftist, Liberal Heathen*. Bloomington, IN: Booktango, 2012.
McClintock, Karen A. *Sexual Shame: An Urgent Call to Healing*. Minneapolis: Augsburg Fortress, 2001.
McGrath, Alister, and Joanna Collicutt McGrath. *The Dawkins Delusion? Atheist Fundamentalism and the Denial of the Divine*. London: SPCK, 2007.
McKenna, George. *The Puritan Origins of American Patriotism*. New Haven: Yale University Press, 2007.
McKim, Robert. *Religious Ambiguity and Religious Diversity*. New York: Oxford University Press, 2001.
McMahon, Darrin M. *Happiness: A History*. New York: Grove/Atlantic, 2006.
Mill, John Stuart. *On Liberty*. Boston: Ticknor and Fields, 1863.
Miller, Steven P. *The Age of Evangelicalism: America's Born-Again Years*. Oxford: Oxford University Press, 2014.
Montgomery, David R. *The Rocks Don't Lie: A Geologist Investigates Noah's Flood*. New York: Norton, 2012.
Morea, Peter C. *Towards a Liberal Catholicism: Psychology and Four Women*. London: SCM, 2000.
Mossner, E. C. *The Life of David Hume*. Oxford: Oxford University Press, 2001.
Moynihan, Robert. *Let God's Light Shine Forth: The Spiritual Vision of Pope Benedict XVI*. New York: Random House, 2005.
Nañez, Rick M. *Full Gospel, Fractured Minds? A Call to Use God's Gift of the Intellect*. Grand Rapids: Zondervan, 2005.
Nehru, Jawaharlal. *Letters from a Father to his Daughter*. New Delhi: Children's Book Trust, 1981.
———. *The Discovery of India*. New Delhi: Nehru Memorial Fund, 1985.
Nelson, James B. *Body Theology*. Louisville: Westminster/John Knox, 1992.
New Covenant Church. "Our Team." Online: http://www.newcovenantsydney.com/about/our-team/.
Nietzsche, Friedrich. *Beyond Good and Evil: Prelude to a Philosophy of the Future*. Cambridge: Cambridge University Press, 2002.
———. *The Gay Science*. New York: Vintage, 1974.
Norman, Larry. "I Wish We'd All Been Ready." On *Only Visiting This Planet*. Verve Records, 1972.

Bibliography

Oberg, Barbara B., and Harry S. Stout. *Benjamin Franklin, Jonathan Edwards, and the Representation of American Culture*. Oxford: Oxford University Press, 1993.
OECD. "Expensive Health Care is Not Always the Best Health Care, Says OECD's Health at a Glance." Online: http://www.oecd.org/health/expensivehealthcare isnotalwaysthebesthealthcaresaysoecdshealthataglance.htm.
O'Neill, Michael. *The Oxford Handbook of Percy Bysshe Shelley*. Oxford: Oxford University Press, 2013.
Oreskes, Naomi, and Erik M. Conway. *Merchants of Doubt: How a Handful of Scientists Obscured the Truth on Issues from Tobacco Smoke to Global Warming*. London: Bloomsbury, 2012.
Pally, Marcia. "The Politics of the 'New Evangelicals': Rethinking Abortion and Gay Marriage." Online: http://www.abc.net.au/religion/articles/2013/02/09/3686782.htm.
Pascal, Blaise. *Pensées*. Mineola, NY: Dover, 2003.
Patrides, C. A. *The Cambridge Platonists*. Cambridge: Cambridge University Press, 1969.
Peaslee, Amos J. *Constitutions of Nations*. Dordrecht: Nijhoff, 1965.
Pelosi, Alexandra. *Friends of God: A Road Trip with Alexandra Pelosi*. New York: HBO: 2007.
Pew Research Center. "Nones on the Rise." Online: http://www.pewforum.org/2012/10/09/nones-on-the-rise/.
Phillips, Paul T. *Kingdom on Earth: Anglo-American Social Christianity, 1880–1940*. University Park, PA: Pennsylvania State University Press, 1996.
Pius XII. "Humani Generis." Online: http://www.vatican.va/holy_father/pius_xii/encyclicals/documents/hf_p-xii_enc_12081950_humani-generis_en.html.
Plato. *The Republic*. Indianapolis: Hackett, 2004.
Poiani, Aldo. *Animal Homosexuality: A Biosocial Perspective*. Cambridge: Cambridge University Press, 2010.
Pomerleau, Wayne P. *Twelve Great Philosophers: A Historical Introduction to Human Nature*. New York: Ardsley, 1997.
Pope, Alexander. *The Poems of Alexander Pope*. Ann Arbor, MI: Sheridan, 1963.
Pope, Stephen J. *Human Evolution and Christian Ethics*. Cambridge: Cambridge University Press, 2007.
Popper, Karl. *Conjectures and Refutations: The Growth of Scientific Knowledge*. London: Routledge Classics, 2002.
Price, Kenneth M. *Walt Whitman: The Contemporary Reviews*. New York: Cambridge University Press, 1996.
Public Religion Research Institute. "Americans Divided over the Fate of Health Care Reform." Online: http://publicreligion.org/research/2012/06/june-religion-politics-2012-research/.
Purdom, Georgia. "Contradictions: How Did Judas Die?" Online: http://www.answersingenesis.org/articles/2009/05/25/contradictions-how-did-judas-die.
Rage Against the Machine. "Vietnow." On *Evil Empire*. Sony Records, 1996.
Ratliff, George. *Hell House*. Los Angeles: Seventh Art Releasing, 2001.
Ratner-Rosenhagen, Jennifer. *American Nietzsche: A History of an Icon and His Ideas*. Chicago: University of Chicago Press, 2012.
Rawls, John. *A Theory of Justice*. Cambridge: Harvard University Press, 2003.

Bibliography

Robinson, Kerry H., et al. *Growing Up Queer: Issues Facing Young Australians Who Are Gender Variant and Sexuality Diverse*. Melbourne: Young and Well Cooperative Research Centre, 2013.

Roemer, Milton I. *National Health Systems of the World: Volume II, The Issues*. Oxford: Oxford University Press, 1993.

Ross, Susan A. "Catholic Women Theologians of the Left." In *What's Left? Liberal American Catholics*, edited by Mary Jo Weaver, 19–45. Bloomington, IN: Indiana University Press, 1999.

Russell, Bertrand. *Unpopular Essays*. New York: Routledge, 2006.

———. *Why I Am Not a Christian: And Other Essays on Religion and Related Subjects*. New York: Simon and Schuster, 1957.

Saad, Lydia. "In U.S., 52% Back Law to Legalize Gay Marriage in 50 States." Online: http://www.gallup.com/poll/163730/back-law-legalize-gay-marriage-states.aspx.

Schindler, D. C. *Hans Urs Von Balthasar and the Dramatic Structure of Truth: A Philosophical Investigation*. New York: Fordham University Press, 2004.

Schopenhauer, Arthur. *Essays of Schopenhauer*. Auckland: Floating, 2010.

Shelley, Percy Bysshe. *The Selected Poetry and Prose of Shelley*. Chatham, UK: Wordsworth, 1994.

Shukla, Bhaskar A. *Feminism: From Mary Wollstonecraft To Betty Friedan*. New Delhi: Sarup and Sons, 2007.

Singer, Peter. "Homosexuality is Not Immoral." Online: http://www.project-syndicate.org/commentary/homosexuality-is-not-immoral#T81gsuJcoiKOyLLU.99

———. *The Expanding Circle: Ethics, Evolution, and Moral Progress*. Princeton: Princeton University Press, 2011.

———. *The Most Good You Can Do: How Effective Altruism Is Changing Ideas about Living Ethically*. New Haven: Yale University Press, 2015.

Soley, Stuart, and Sasha Hadden. "The LGBT Apology." Online: http://www.pozible.com/project/182832

Sommer, Volker, and Paul L. Vasey. *Homosexual Behaviour in Animals: An Evolutionary Perspective*. Cambridge: Cambridge University Press, 2006.

Spong, John Shelby. *Rescuing the Bible from Fundamentalism*. New York: HarperCollins, 1992.

———. *Why Christianity Must Change or Die*. New York: HarperCollins, 1999.

Statistics Canada. "2011 National Household Survey: Immigration, Place of Birth, Citizenship, Ethnic Origin, Visible Minorities, Language and Religion." Online: http://www.statcan.gc.ca/daily-quotidien/130508/dq130508b-eng.htm?HPA.

Stewart, Cynthia. *The Catholic Church: A Brief Popular History*. Terrace Heights, WA: St Mary's Press, Christian Brothers Publications, 2008.

Sullivan, Roger J. *Immanuel Kant's Moral Theory*. Cambridge: Cambridge University Press, 1995.

Summers, Anne. *The Misogyny Factor*. Sydney: University of New South Wales Press, 2012.

Taylor, Barbara. "The Religious Foundations of Mary Wollstonecraft's Feminism." In *The Cambridge Companion to Mary Wollstonecraft*, edited by Claudia L. Johnson, 99–118. Cambridge: Cambridge University Press, 2002.

Tent, James F. *In the Shadow of the Holocaust: Nazi Persecution of Jewish-Christian Germans*. Lawrence, KS: University Press of Kansas, 2003.

Bibliography

Tertullian. *The Selected Works of Tertullian Quintus Septimius Florens Tertullianus.* OrthodoxEbook, 2010.

Theols, Philo. *Divine Sex: Liberating Sex from Religious Tradition.* Bloomington, IN: Trafford, 2003.

Thomas, Choo. *Heaven Is So Real.* Lake Mary, FL: Charisma House, 2006.

Thornton, Tim. *Wittgenstein on Language and Thought.* Edinburgh: Edinburgh University Press, 1998.

Thorpe, Ian, and Robert Wainwright. *This is Me: The Autobiography.* London: Simon and Schuster, 2012.

Treays, Jane. *The Virgin Daughters.* Manchester: Granada Television, 2008.

Tuck, William Powell. *The Left Behind Fantasy: The Theology behind the Left Behind Tales.* Eugene, OR: Resource, 2010.

Turner, Paul. "The Order of Mass: Comforting Words." In *Lift Up Your Hearts: A Pastoral, Theological, and Historical Survey of the Third Typical Edition of the Roman Missal*, edited by Robert L. Tuzik, 63–76. Chicago: Archdiocese of Chicago, 2011.

Utter, Glenn H. *Mainline Christians and U.S. Public Policy: A Reference Handbook.* Santa Barbara, CA: ABC-CLIO, 2007.

Venn-Brown, Anthony. *A Life of Unlearning: A Journey to Find the Truth.* Sydney: New Holland, 2007.

Villa, Dana. *The Cambridge Companion to Hannah Arendt.* Cambridge: Cambridge University Press, 2000.

Vines, Matthew. *God and the Gay Christian.* New York: Doubleday, 2014.

———. "The Gay Debate." Online: http://www.youtube.com/watch?v=ezQjNJUSraY

Walker, Grace. *Women Are Defective Males: The Calculated Denigration of Women by the Catholic Church and its Disastrous Consequences Today.* Sandy, UT: Aardvark Global, 2010.

Wauzzinski, Robert A. *Between God and Gold: Protestant Evangelicalism and the Industrial Revolution: 1820–1914.* Cranbury, NJ: Associated Universities Press, 1993.

Welker, Michael. "Sola Scriptura? The Authority of the Bible in Pluralistic Environments." In *A God So Near: Essays on Old Testament Theology in Honor of Patrick D. Miller*, edited by Brent A. Strawn and Nancy R. Bowen, 374–92. Wiona Lake, IN: Eisenbrauns, 2003.

Westphal, Merold. *Suspicion and Faith: The Religious Uses of Modern Atheism.* New York: Fordham University Press, 2004.

White Jr., Ronald C. *Lincoln's Greatest Speech: The Second Inaugural.* New York: Simon and Schuster, 2002.

Wiestad, Else. "Empowerment Inside Patriarchy: Rousseau and the Masculine Construction of Femininity" In *Feminist Interpretations of Jean-Jacques Rousseau*, edited by Lynda Lange, 169–86. University Park: Pennsylvania State University Press, 2002.

Wiley, Tatha. "Humanae Vitae: Sexual Ethics and the Roman Catholic Church." In *The Embrace of Eros: Bodies, Desires, and Sexuality in Christianity*, edited by Margaret D. Kamitsuka, 99–114. Minneapolis: Fortress, 2010.

Williams, Bernard. *The Sense of the Past: Essays in the History of Philosophy.* Princeton: Princeton University Press, 2006.

Wilson, Emily. *The Death of Socrates.* London: Profile, 2007

Wisener, Merry. "Luther and Women: The Death of Two Marys." In *Feminist Theology: A Reader*, edited by Ann Loades, 123–37. London: SPCK, 1990.

Wollstonecraft, Mary. *A Vindication of the Rights of Men and a Vindication of the Rights of Women*. Cambridge: Cambridge University Press, 1995.
Žižek, Slavoj. *Violence: Six Sideways Reflections*. London: Profile, 2009.
Zuckerman, Phil. *Atheism and Secularity*. Santa Barbara, CA: Greenwood, 2010.

Name/subject Index

666, (See Number of the Beast)

A Thief in the Night (film), 136–37
Abortion, 13, 52, 73–76, 141, 145
Abstinence, 29–33, 39–41
Answers in Genesis, 21, 23
Anti-Intellectualism, 12–14
Aristotle, 4, 6, 67, 94, 99
Australian Christian Lobby, 58

Barker, Dan, 76
Beauvoir, Simon de, 5, 100–108
Bernardi, Cory, 62
Biblical literalism, See Literalism
Blackburn, Simon, 133

Calvary Chapel, 17
Carson, Ben, 49–50
Catholicism, 3, 7, 14, 103, 116, 138
    Attitudes to abortion, 73
    Attitudes to divorce, 70
    Attitudes to evolution, 91–92
    Attitudes to homosexuality, 48–49, 52–54
    Attitudes to women, 99, 106–8
    Catholic guilt, 37
    Church attendance, 46
    Connection to Liberal Party of Australia, 32, 58, 62, 116
    Liberal and authoritarian wings, 158
    On Biblical literalism, 23, 26, 84, 106–8
    Response to Obamacare, 114
Chairman Mao, See Zedong, Mao
Charismatic movement, 2, 12, 16, 92, 129, 137
Christian Fundamentalism, See Fundamentalism
Christian Left, 145–47
Christian Right, 14, 28, 32–33, 46, 62, 64, 73, 86, 113–14, 119–20, 144–47
Communism, 113, 121
Council of Mâcon, 99
Creation Science, 86

Dawkins, Richard, 9, 157
Deontology, 68–79
Dispensational theology, See End Times Genre
Divine Sex (book), See Philo Thelos
Divorce, 59, 69–70

Eco, Umberto, 72
End Times Genre, 137–40
Evangelicalism, 3, 7, 12, 14, 23, 26, 77, 124, 138, 140, 142
    Attitudes to abortion, 73
    Attitudes to homosexuality, 48–49, 54
    Attitudes to sex, 30–32, 37

173

Name/subject Index

Evangelicalism (*continued*)
    Divorce rate, 70
    Growth rate, 16–17
Eve, 98
Evolution, 14, 25, 82–94, 130
    Scopes Trial, 85–86, 138

Falwell, Jerry, 140, 142, 146
Female Priests, 103–4
Feminism, 33, 97, 103
    Biblical misogyny, 97–100
    Feminist existentialism, 101–2
    Women's Movement, 97
Flood Myth, See Noah's Flood
Freire, Paulo, 130–31
Friends of God (film), 127–28
Frisbee, Lonnie, 17
Fundamentalism, 2
    Early history, 12–13
    Response to science, 85–86
    Opposition to Fundamentalism, 154–55
    World's Christian Fundamentalist Association, 12, 85

Global Atheist Convention, 1–2, 11
Gorgias, 74
God and the Gay Christian (book), See Vines, Matthew
God is Not Great (book), See Hitchens, Christopher
God's Not Dead (film), 4–5, 130
Gould, Stephen Jay, 82
Gundry, Robert, 19

Hegel, Georg Wilhelm Friedrich, 67–68, 101, 111, 113
Hell House, 140–42
Hillsong,
    Church, 3, 18, 38, 53–54, 64, 108, 129
    College, 65, 108
    Houston, Bobbie, 36, 107
    Houston, Brian, 17, 54, 107
Hitchens, Christopher, vii, 9, 125, 154
Hitler, Adolf, 45

Hobbes, Thomas, 21, 24, 140
Holyoake, George Jacob, 142–43
Homeschooling, 129–31
Homophobia, See LGBTIQ
Houston, Brian, See Hillsong
Houston, Bobbie, See Hillsong
Hume, David, 5, 23–25, 69

Intelligent Design, See Creation Science

Jesus Movement, 17–18

Kant, Immanuel, 69

Lakewood Church, 18
    Osteen, Joel, 18, 108
    Osteen, Victoria, 108
Le Deuxième Sexe (book), See Beauvoir, Simone de
Left Behind (films), 134–36
Left Behind (books), 134–36, 139
Lewis. C. S., 76
Literalism, 18–23, 25–27
LGBTIQ,
    Affirming churches, 53, 64
    Christian attitudes, 46, 52–55, 58–62, 73
    Comparison to atheism, 50–51
    Homophobia, 42–43, 49–50, 56–57
    In popular culture, 47
    Marriage Equality, 46, 59–62
    Suicide, 52
Luther, Martin, 19
Luxemburg, Rosa, 119–21

Marriage Equality, See LGBTIQ
Marx, Karl, 5, 110–13, 121–22
Marxism, 20, 120–23
May, Rollo, 158
Mega-Church, 18, 45
Mencken, Henry Louis, 12–14, 85–86
Mere Christianity (book), 76
Mill, John Stuart, 5, 55–66, 70–71
Moral Relativism, See Relativism

Name/subject Index

Morea, Peter, C., 158

Nazism, 45, 59, 138
Nehru, Jawaharlal, 126–27, 132
New Atheism, 8–10
Nietzsche, Friedrich, 9, 15, 74–78, 111, 153–54
Noah's Flood, 21–23
Noah (film), 21–22
Number of the Beast, 19

Obama, Barack, 28, 57, 114, 146
    Obamacare, 119
O'Hair, Madalyn Murray, 129
Osteen, Joel, See Lakewood Church
Osteen, Victoria, See Lakewood Church

Palin, Sarah, 28–29
Pascal, Blaise, 155–56
Pedagogies of the Oppressed (book), See Paulo Freire
Pelosi, Alexandra, 127
Pentecostalism, 3, 12, 14, 16–17, 39, 53–54, 92, 124, 129
Peretti, Frank, 138
Philosopher King, 150
Popper, Karl, viii, 87–90, 94
Purity Balls, 30–31

Rawls, John, 117–119
Religious Right, (see Christian Right)
Relativism, 71–72
Russell, Bertrand, vii, 5, 143–44, 159

Same-Sex Marriage, See LGBTIQ
Schopenhauer, Arthur, 15–16
Science and Religion, 80–86
Scopes Trial, See Evolution
Secularization, 7
Shelley, Mary, 35
Shelley, Percy Bysshe, 35, 41, 151

Singer, Peter, 51–52, 78
Smith, Chuck, See Calvary Chapel
Socrates, 148–52
    Similarities to Jesus Christ, 151
Spong, John Shelby, 154
St Paul,
    Apostle, 2, 26, 36, 97–99, 101, 105–9
    Cathedral, 17
St Peter, 2
St Thomas Aquinas, 6–7, 94, 99
Stalin, Joseph, 9, 44–45, 121
Summa Theologica (book), 6
Suspicion and Faith (book), 111

Tertullian, 4, 94, 98, 152
Thales of Miletus, 4
Thelos, Philo, 39–40
The God Delusion (book), See Dawkins, Richard
The Most Good You Can Do (book), 78
Thorpe, Ian, 42

Universal Healthcare, 113–17
Venn-Brown, Anthony, 64
Vineyard Church, 17
Vines, Matthew, 54–55

Westphal, Merold, 111
Wilde, Oscar, 156
Wilson, E.O., 51–52
Witch Hunts, 99–100
Wittgenstein, Ludwig, 149
Woolstonecraft, Mary, 33–35

Young earth creationism, 86, 89, 93

Zacharias, Ravi, viii, 25
Zedong, Mao, 9, 44–45, 121
Žižek, Slavoj, 86–87

Scripture Index

OLD TESTAMENT

Genesis

1:1–27	20
2:1–20	20
2:18	105
3:16	96

Exodus

20:17	104

2 Samuel

12:1–7a	118

Proverbs

3:13–15	ix
8:1–11	148
8:11	10

NEW TESTAMENT

Matthew

5:1	20
5:3	20
22:37–39	63
24:36–44	137
27:5	20

Luke

6:17	20
21:1–4	112

John

1:23	72
6:53–54	26
8:32	152
8:37	152

Acts

26:2	2
1:18	21

1 Corinthians

9:27	36
11:5	99
11:7	99
11:10	26
13:13	155
14:34	26

Ephesians

5:22–33	105
6:5	26

Colossians

3:22	26

1 Timothy

2:10	26
2:11–13	99
2:14	97

2 Timothy

3:16	23

1 Peter

3:15	2

Revelation

13:18	19

www.ingramcontent.com/pod-product-compliance
Lightning Source LLC
Chambersburg PA
CBHW071231170426
43191CB00032B/1311